ENDORSEMENTS

"My sippicup is overflowing from all the wisdom, practical ideas, real-life stories, and illustrations!"

—Pam Farrel
codirector of Farrel Communications, Masterful Living Ministries

"*A Car Seat in My Convertible?* will touch your heart, tickle your funny bone, and provide plenty of practical help for being the grandmother you've always wanted to be."

—Karen O'Connor
author of *Gettin' Old Ain't for Wimps* and *The Beauty of Aging*

"More than money in the bank or expensive heirlooms, a godly heritage and simple memories are the treasures that will have eternal significance. A must-read for all grandmothers who desire to leave a godly legacy for generations to come."

—Sharon Jaynes
author of *Being a Great Mom, Raising Great Kids*

"Dig into the wit and wisdom of this book and begin to make this season of life the most important and productive one ever!"

—Lucinda Secrest McDowell
author of *Role of a Lifetime*

"Sharon has penned a spiritual guidebook that makes the grandparenting adventure an exciting journey with twists and turns down paths of wisdom and grace."

—**Allison Bottke**
author of *Setting Boundaries with Your Adult Children,* and
founder of God Allows U-Turns

God is using Sharon and her message to fill a much needed gap. She is helping grandmothers and grandmothers-to-be to live out their special role effectively using their time, acceptance, prayers, and faith.

—**Jennifer Rothschild**
author of *Lessons I Learned in the Dark* and *Self Talk Soul Talk*

A CAR SEAT IN MY CONVERTIBLE?

SHARON HOFFMAN

GIVING YOUR GRANDKIDS
THE SPIRITUAL RIDE *of*
THEIR LIVES

A CAR SEAT IN MY CONVERTIBLE?

SHARON HOFFMAN

GIVING YOUR GRANDKIDS
THE SPIRITUAL RIDE *of*
THEIR LIVES

NEW HOPE
PUBLISHERS
Birmingham Alabama

New Hope® Publishers
P. O. Box 12065
Birmingham, AL 35202-2065
www.newhopepublishers.com
New Hope Publishers is a division of WMU®

Library of Congress Cataloging-in-Publication Data

Hoffman, Sharon.
  A car seat in my convertible? : giving your grandkids the spiritual ride of their lives / Sharon Hoffman.
    p. cm.
  Includes bibliographical references.
  ISBN 978-1-59669-208-4 (sc)
  1. Grandparents--Prayers and devotions. 2. Grandchildren--Religious life. I. Title.
BV4845.H64 2008
248.8'45--dc22
                    2007050443

ISBN-10: 1-59669-208-1
ISBN-13: 978-1-59669-208-4

N084134• 0508 • 5M1

DEDICATION

To my Pure-Gold Grandchildren:
Ellie, Anna, Jake, Audrey, Faith, and Caleb

CONTENTS

Foreword *by Carol Kent* 12

Acknowledgments 13

Introduction 15

Chapter 1
ESTABLISH YOUR STYLE 17

Chapter 2
GIVE LOVE THAT NEVER FAILS..25

Chapter 3
BATHE THEM IN PRAYER 31

Chapter 4
CHOOSE TO LEAVE A LEGACY..39

Chapter 5
CREATE PRAYER TOOLS—JOURNAL, GUIDE, AND CALENDAR 45

Chapter 6
BLESSED ARE THE GRANDMOMS WHO MAKE TIME........................51

Chapter 7
ENCOURAGE EFFECTIVELY..57

Chapter 8
BE REMEMBERED AS A FUN, GUTSY GRANDMOM...........................65

Chapter 9
STRENGTHEN RELATIONSHIPS THROUGH PLAY.............................73

Chapter 10
Tell Jokes, Spin Tales, and Maintain Joy....................................81

Chapter 11
Take 29 Tips from Veteran Grandmoms.................................91

Chapter 12
Never Give Up on Your Grandchildren—or Their Parents............113

Chapter 13
Rebuild for the Future...121

Chapter 14
Dare to Surrender Everything.......................................131

Chapter 15
Leave a Legacy of Spiritual Heirlooms 139

Chapter 16
Make a Difference—and Let Them Watch 147

Chapter 17
Prioritize Purity...155

Chapter 18
Bestow an Eternal Heritage...161

Bibliography...165

FOREWORD

Humor author Theresa Bloomingdale once said, "If your baby is beautiful and perfect, never cries or fusses, sleeps on schedule and burps on demand, is an angel all the time—you're the grandma." At this stage in my life, nothing brings me more pleasure than spending time with my granddaughters. Their photographs are in my wallet and their drawings on my refrigerator. I pray for them every day and envision what they might be when they grow up.

Having taught speech and drama, I look forward to their stage productions, where I am an audience of one applauding their puppet shows and cheering after their living room musical performances. Naturally, I'm quite certain that my granddaughters are as close to professional actresses as children can be and I am convinced their IQs are extraordinarily high.

If I'm prejudiced, it's because I am a grandma. I know they are the smartest, most well-behaved, prettiest, and charming of all children. They're mine! And I long to make a lasting impact on their lives.

Sharon Hoffman has written a book that made me laugh and cry—and she reminded me that I don't have to be perfect to be a good grandma. Psychologist and philosopher William James once said, "The great use of life is to spend it on something that will outlast it." If you have ever questioned how to make a vivid, personal, deeply spiritual impression on the lives of your grandchildren—whether they are infants or teenagers—*A Car Seat in My Convertible?* is the tool you need to be a grandmother who will leave a lasting legacy for your grandkids.

Carol Kent, speaker and author
A New Kind of Normal and
When I Lay My Isaac Down

ACKNOWLEDGMENTS

There are 100-plus friends and family members from all over the globe who have given of their hearts to allow me to share their real-life stories within the pages of this book. I affectionately thank you all for touching my life deeply. You've helped me not to lose sight of what a special and important role grandmoms have in the life of a grandchild.

Special thanks go to Myrtle Ross, Sue Garard, Mary Buckner, and Oleta Midgett—you believed and in supported this work with never-ending encouragement from beginning to end.

Midge Doelling, your coming to my aid whenever I cried "Help!" will never be forgotten.

A big thanks goes to my monthly writers group. Amy, Penny, Sue, Nancy—your encouragement and many cups of tea have helped me run this race with endurance. I wouldn't have even gotten off the starting line without you girls.

May praise and blessings be especially upon the head of Amy Reed for believing in this project when no one else did. Thank you for your untiring efforts in providing such magical editing touches. I believe God broke the mold when He made you.

Andrea Mullins and Joyce Dinkins—thank you for illuminating the way. What fun it is to be making a difference for Jesus in this world with you beautiful women at New Hope.

My husband, Rob, you are the best person in the whole world to do life with. I absolutely could not love you more. Thank you for every encouragement, sacrifice, hug, smile, prayer, and for bringing me chocolate during my months of writing. What an honor it is to be your wife.

INTRODUCTION

The day my daughter and son-in-love (that's what I like to call him) told me their home pregnancy test was positive, I first understood what it means to be a member of the exclusive and extraordinary club called "Grandmotherhood." Like grandmas do, I was filled with an enormous sense of wonder at what God had in store for this precious new life. I wanted to tell the world—or at least five of my close friends who were showing me pictures of their little darlings already. Amazingly, now *my* daughter was having a daughter *of her very own*. No wonder my already-members-of-the-club friends had thought I just didn't get it. There were no words to describe my elation.

My heart, however, was not emotionally prepared for the many good-byes I would experience over the next years with three of my grandchildren who live a great distance from me. Sometimes I miss them till I ache, especially after sweet visits of sharing laughter and building memories. There are always tearful departures.

It was after one such especially joyful visit that God placed the idea for this book in my heart. Blinking back tears, I halfheartedly sank into my assigned airplane seat, 17C window, exit row. That's exactly what I longed to do. Exit the airplane. Our visit had been far too short.

Everything within me wanted to run back through the terminal to my precious granddaughter Ellie's outstretched hands. Only as I'd rounded the last curve in the security line had I dared look back toward my daughter holding her. Tightly clutching the pink blanket I'd made for her, Ellie spontaneously flung herself forward in my direction and began to wail, as if pleading, "Nana, why can't I come with you?" Wiping her eyes, the security screener had told me she couldn't watch the scene any longer; she had had to look away.

On that flight home, I held on to a picture of Ellie as if it were a life preserver. To someone who is not yet a grandmother, the only way I could describe it is to say it's like falling in love again. Living hundreds of miles away from my first grandchild was not easy. The aching loneliness to hold or tuck her into bed at night under the soft pink fleece blanket was ever-present.

But from my experience that day, I had a flash of godly inspiration that changed everything for me as a grandmother. I want to share it with you. As I had watched two little waving hands grow smaller and smaller as I walked down the terminal, I had sensed God's reassurance in my heart: *No matter how great the distance, Sharon, through Me there are loving ways you can blanket your grandchildren in love each and every day.* It had been one of those pay-attention-to-God moments. Right there in my exit row, I scribbled down the word *blanket* on my airline napkin. With a heartfelt determination, I vowed then and there to cover my grandchildren with valuable truths—to instill in them something much bigger than the here and now. Each letter of the word stood for an action I could take. My legacy to them would be assurances of my love for and faith in God that I would share with them.

Through the years since, as I've continued my ministry of speaking to and writing for women, I have received additional inspiration from God on how special my role in my grandchildren's lives can be. It was as if He were laying within me a foundation to share with others. I began reaching out, forming a network of more than a hundred other like-minded grandmoms to learn the secrets, tips, and insights they had. The result, which I share with you now, is the premise of the book that began on that airplane that jetted me away from my granddaughter:

B—Bathe your grandchildren in prayer.
L—Love, live, and laugh often with your grands!
A—Accept, affirm, and appreciate each grandchild unconditionally.
N—Never give up on your grandchildren—or their parents.
K—Keep expressing assurances of your love.
E—Establish your own style of grandmothering.
T—Take the time to leave a spiritual legacy.

Funny how one word changed the direction of my life that day. But it has. Forever. Now it is my prayer that it will do the same for you. I long to inspire other grandmothers to join me on my quest—to be great grandmothers. We all can have an impact on our grandchildren for eternity. Simply put, that is the concept of this book. With the help of 100 of my close friends, you'll find these pages full of some helpful new ideas, heartwarming stories, and many answers to grandmothers' prayers.

I've heard many grown-ups say, looking back over their lives, that a special grandmother was the guiding light of their lives. The goal of this book is to help you find your personal style in being a godly grandma. While I may not take each letter in the word *blanket* in order, the spirit of each letter is addressed to help grandmoms *and* children all over the world to achieve their God-given potential. Covering your precious bundles of potential with a love that's wrapped in fervent prayers, you can make a tremendous difference for today and all eternity.

This world could use a lot more women who commit to do this. And I'll bet there's a child in your life who could use a woman who will. I know there is in mine.

ESTABLISH YOUR STYLE

Each of us will establish our own style of grandmothering. My convertible not only has a car seat in the back, but it also has gear that appeals to toddlers, such as books, toys, and yummy snacks stashed in the console. As well, there are most often crumbs strewn all over the back floor mats. Ah, leftover impressions of a cracker-crunching child's recent presence. As much as I enjoy cruising in a clean car, I wouldn't trade those evidences of my grandchildren for anything in the world! There is nothing that gives me more pleasure than spending time with them, knowing that I have one more opportunity to make an investment in their lives. Looking up in the rearview mirror to see a little towheaded toddler with a smile on his or her face helps to remind me that I'm not living for only today, I'm spending my life investing in eternity. I hope this book will inspire you to do the same.

Since becoming a grandmom, I find myself reading every grandparent book I can get my hands on. I observe other grandmothers in malls, the grocery market, at church, everywhere I go. How do I find them, you ask? I don't have to look for them. We seem to find each other. Who but a grandmother would walk up to a child in a restaurant in a high chair and tickle, coo, and ask how old he is so that she might better tell the size of her own grandchild? (Yes, I admit I've been guilty of that more than once.)

You *know* you're with a grandmother comrade when you're out shopping with a friend and you both walk straight to the children's department. I knew I had joined the sisterhood the first time I walked right past the women's shoe sale toward the sign marked *Infant Clothing Sale*. Of course, I credit the extra expenses on my check card at the end of the month as a surefire way to earn those frequent-flyer miles the card pays to be used toward additional grandchildren trips. ("Think of the money I'm saving on flights, husband," I contend convincingly while unloading the trunk.)

It was hard to imagine how grandchildren would change every aspect of my life. Oh, but they have. While I relish in the joys, I sometimes find it difficult to keep up with their antics, juggle the travel it takes to carve out visits, and find creative ways to do *my* own thing once in a while without guilt-tripping. Maybe you understand exactly what I mean and there are days when you feel the same way. That's why I've gathered together more than 100 women from all over the world to help out with this book. They are an absolutely darling gaggle of friends who are completely "today's grandmoms." They have teamed with me as I've written and we've become a part of a heartfelt sisterhood while partnering in prayer, pictures, progress, giggles, advice, apprehensions, and tears too. I hope you will gain great joy from reading their amazing stories. Their wisdom and experience demonstrate that the eternal joys of being a grandmother far outweigh any burden, especially if we support one another. Many of us have been able to avoid unnecessary mistakes and difficulties by dipping into the well of each others' strengths.

To become a grandmother is to fling open a brand-new door.

THE POWER OF ONE

How about you? How has grandmotherhood changed your life? To become a grandmother is to fling open a brand-new door. To grow. To share experiences and valued knowledge among women in a way that forms a bond of sisterhood like no other. When I was a little girl, grandmothers were old women with white hair, wrinkles, and dresses that buttoned down the front. They were proper baking experts who smelled like lilacs and wore hosiery even when they gardened or cleaned the house. To me, they were *elderly*. I think that is why some of us have a hard time transitioning into becoming a grandmom because we may think, *But, I'm not that old!* Grandmothering was a prototype we had always associated with old age.

We grandmothers of today are different entirely, so what we need is an updated view of today's grandmothers, for today's women. That's why we need this book—

and each other. Grandmothering is no longer the way it was and the role does not *look* the way it once looked. Baby boomers have totally redefined the definition. We need common-sense, experience-tested, grandmothering-in-the-real-world role clarification. Don't despair; I promise you this book is not full of we-know-it-all, pushy platitudes. What it does contain are many ways to help make your grandmothering more useful, less stressful, and more joyful.

Every time we turn on the news, we hear of one more account of another troubled person who has done some terrible thing. Just this past week while writing, my heart broke at news of another horrific shooting on a college campus. Several reports made mention to the shooter's childhood as a loner. His family commented sadly about him being constantly "tormented by loneliness." So often that seems to be said of those who commit heinous crimes. Yet, you can look at families where parents abused or neglected the children, and mysteriously, some turn out to be secure, solid citizens and others do not. The upbringing of a child matters enormously, but it is obviously not the sole reasoning for the outcome of a child into adulthood. Consider the following comment:

> "When you look at a hundred people whose younger years were miserable, you'll find that among them there are survivors, people who were able to come through childhoods of torment and become fine adults. This isn't a matter of luck. From careful research we've learned that what these survivors usually have in common is that as children they had at least one grown-up they could count on."
> —Suzette Haden Elgin, The *Grandmother Principles*

Notice again those words: "one grown-up they could count on." Loving grandmothers have never been more desperately needed. Children today are looking for sincere love. We can fill the space of that one grown-up in a child's life who cares and who loves.

One dear friend of mine, Myrtle, has opened her home and her heart to a precious grandson these past five years. With his parents divorcing, little Aaron needed a secure place to call home. Myrtle's home enfolds him with loving comfort and care. "What else could I do? This little fella is my reason for living! He's why I fought so hard to get well when I had pneumonia," Myrtle told me one morning with eyes brimming with tears.

As a result, Aaron is soaking up that love—and it is changing his life. There's not a Sunday that I don't see the two of them walking into our church together. I believe Myrtle's crown in heaven is going to be full of precious jewels for the loving sacrifices she is making for her dear grandson. The authentic, encouraging love of this grandmom really has made a difference.

We all have had "Red Sea" moments in our lives. You know, situations when we're certain we will drown unless God moves on our behalf. Then He brings someone into our life as a lifeline for us, often just before all appears lost. You may be the *only* grown-up your grandchild has today to truly count on to toss out an inner tube. The message is simple. Be who God calls *you* to be. Your most important opportunity to love in life may show up when you least expect it. Sometimes, ready or not, it is in the life of a grandchild.

> Nobody can do for little children what grandparents do. Grandparents sort of sprinkle stardust over the lives of little children.
> —Alex Haley

Pedicures and Hot Chai Tea Lattes

As I crisscross the nation speaking to women, those who are grandmothers gravitate to my book table, where I just so happen to have a photo album of my family (in case they need to see my grandchildren!). It's always fun to share my photos, but ultimately I've found that a deeper joy has been viewing other grandmoms' pride and joys. I love listening to ways women are taking on this challenging, exciting role of grandmothering and finding their own way of doing things. While there is no proven recipe for success, I have listened with great interest to the increased self-awareness that comes with being a grandmother. One woman summed it up this way:

> Becoming a grandma has made me know myself a lot better. I give up control much more freely, understand my family members in deeper ways, and my daughter-in-law and I are developing a stronger relationship. We had a stormy start, but now we're actually enjoying family get-togethers. I find myself much more forgiving and less critical now that a child's feelings are to be considered. I like myself and everyone else better these days. I guess my pride kept me from reaching out much before. Now that there's a child to consider, I don't hesitate.

That's so important to remember! Little did I know how much I'd need all the wisdom I'm gleaning from so many wise women. Three years ago, my daughter and son-in-love asked me if I would make space for babysitting my grandchild on Monday and Thursday mornings. Gathering the best mothering skills I could muster, I felt honored and up to the challenge.

There I was, the eager-to-be grandmother, ready to do whatever or whenever even before my little sweetheart could ask. While most of the care in my home two mornings a week has gone smoothly (it's kind of like riding a bicycle—you never forget how to care for an infant; it all comes back to you) there has, however, been a certain amount of adjusting and apprehension.

There are good reasons for this. I work out of my home office and have had to discover how to care for someone else's child in my own home. I'd never done that before. I don't mind admitting that there are those times when sitting all morning for a spa pedicure with my feet up as I sip a hot chai tea latte sounds really good (especially Monday mornings after I've been traveling all weekend). Oh, but I wouldn't trade the sweet, sacred moments that twice-a-week *play dates* with my grandchildren have given me (that's what we've lovingly opted to call *babysitting time*) for all the serenity or teatime in the world.

It's kind of like riding a bicycle—you never forget how to care for an infant!

I've concluded that, as much as I loved being a mom to my two daughters, I was way too preoccupied with day-to-day life to enjoy some of the simple, sweet moments. I'm getting to do that now with my grandchildren: being with them for moments like on a recent walk when three-year-old Jake bent over to pull the top of a dandelion flower off its stem. Leaning over a second time, he tried to attach the fluffy flower back onto its upright green stem. I'll never forget the pleading in his eyes when he looked up at me and said, "Fikx it, Nana." I wish I could have. As I showed him how that was not possible, I realized that there will be many situations all through Jake's life Nana won't be able to "fikx," no matter how hard I try. Children instinctively teach us, don't they?

Just yesterday morning I had the privilege of snuggling my granddaughter to sleep. After reading four favorite books to her with our lullaby music playing softly in the background, little one-year-old Faith surrendered peacefully to her morning nap. Soothed by her melodic breathing, I sank back into our overstuffed sofa to relish in the momentary island of calm. I mused silently to myself about how quickly I've become enchanted with this little rosy-cheeked darling. "Piggying" her tiny toes, playing peekaboo, singing a lullaby, giving horsy rides...I snapped a picture to put in my heart. She may not remember these special times on my sofa. That's OK. I will never forget. It's because of such sweet memories forever embedded deep in this grandma's heart that I've chosen these words as my life verses for this season of my life:

We will not hide them from their children, telling to the generation to come the praises of the LORD, and His strength and His wonderful works that He has done . . . . that the generation to come might know them, the children who would be born, that they may arise and declare them to their children.
—Psalm 78:4, 6

Fix these words of mine in your hearts and minds; tie them as symbols on your hands and bind them on your foreheads. Teach them to your children, talking about them when you sit at home and when you walk along the road, when you lie down and when you get up.
—Deuteronomy 11:18–19 (NIV)

Someone once said, "It is much more important to be significant in someone's life than to be successful." I agree—that's the key to happiness! Making a difference in the life of a grandchild gives us a priceless purpose for living.

As Sheila Kitzinger says in *Becoming a Grandmother*, most grandmothers, like mothers, do not step into their roles as instant stars. We *learn* to be grandmothers just as we learned to be mothers.

TAKING BACK THE GRAND

After Rebecca Smith of Petal, Mississippi, and I chatted about our grands together, I asked her to write down her charming experience. She sent me the following:

I was trying, without success, to settle my three-year-old grandson down for a nap. He was agitating his sister and fighting the sleep process. I told him he must obey me and quiet down for his rest. His parents were at a jewelry trade show and I was "in charge" for the day. I told him, "If you do not settle down, I will have to punish you and that is not my job." He lay down, squinted his eyes thoughtfully at me and said, "Well, Gram, what is your job?" Some words came out of my mouth and he settled down and napped. As I left the room I began to really ponder, *What exactly is my job with my grandchildren?*

What I've learned from hearing stories from grandmothers and about grandmothers is that there is no set-in-stone job description. Whatever your style, find it; navigate your own course. Avoid the trap of comparing yourself with your grandchild's other grandparents, by letting God show you the special skills *you* have to offer. Want to establish your own style of grandmothering? Become a woman of faith, acceptance, and above all these...love.

GIVE LOVE THAT NEVER FAILS 2

W e've all asked ourselves that question. What do grandmothers *do?* What I'm learning is that the most powerful thing we can do as grandmoms is to love. I've heard it time and time again, "The most powerful thing while I was growing up is that I knew my grandmother would always love me, no matter what happens." Those words from 25-year-old Chris did not refer to the kind of "convenience love" children grow up with, for example, as they watch TV as a substitute for one-on-one attention. Hardly. What this young man was pointing out to me was a genuine, committed, "I will love you no matter what," unconditional love that survives all things through all time. I think that's what he meant when I said, "Tell me about your grandmother" and the first words out of his mouth were, "Oh, my grandmother is *grand!*" You should have seen his eyes light up when he spoke about her. A sight to behold!

Whatever it is that we do as grandmoms, it is imperative that we communicate love. More than knowledge, more than skills, more than coaching, more than changing diapers...love is most important.

My heart's desire is that a message of love comes across when I say to each of our grandchildren at bedtime and at partings, "I love you as high as the sky and as deep as the ocean." This little singsong saying has become our thing. My grands anticipate it when I lean in close to tuck them in. When they recite it back without reservation or hesitation, how my heart is lifted. Every hug, every prayer, every word motivates me to show love in the best way I know how.

I must always remember, though, in order for me to love well, I must let God love *me.* It is only when we accept God's love that we can let His love flow through us.

When our own love cup is full, it can't help but overflow to our families. God's love is the greatest gift we can give.

> *Love suffers long and is kind, love does not envy; love does not parade itself, is not puffed up; does not behave rudely, does not seek its own, is not provoked, thinks no evil; does not rejoice in iniquity, but rejoices in the truth; bears all things, believes all things, hopes all things, endures all things. Love never fails.*
> —1 Corinthians 13:4–8.

THERE'S ONLY ONE YOU

You are a valuable representative of the God who created you. Being a grandmom is a crucial role in His kingdom. You are a child of the Most High God. When God created you, He also designed a specific purpose for you alone to accomplish at this particular place and time in history. Even if your grandchildren have two or more grandmothers in addition to you, God longs for you to be a representative of His love to the children that He has placed in your life.

All grandmothers are special, but very different from each other. You are as unique as your grandchildren are. No two grandmoms are just alike and not every grandmother faces the same set of circumstances. God wants you to be *your* personal best. After all, you are the apple of His eye. Knowing who you are in Christ and who He is in you gives all the confidence you'll ever need to be all that you can be for your grandchildren. You are God's beloved masterpiece. Talk about a surefire method to bolster your confidence! I'm confident that if we first let God love *us* well, then we will be able to love our children and grandchildren well.

I SHALL NOT LIVE IN VAIN
If I can stop one heart from breaking,
I shall not live in vain;
If I can ease one life the aching,
Or cool one pain,
Or help one fainting robin
Unto his nest again,
I shall not live in vain.
—Emily Dickinson

THE RELUCTANT GRANDMOTHER

Whether you have 1 grandchild or 21, the news of a new grandchild always brings with it anticipation and questions. You may even have myriad reasons why you are not quite ready to be a grandmom. Reactions to the news of impending grandparenthood vary greatly, depending on your circumstances. Not every grandmom I've met has been excited to meet the newest member of the family clan. This is understandable.

Answers to my question when I polled 100 grandmoms included "excited, elated, nervous, shocked, scared, overjoyed, apprehensive, ecstatic, angry, not sure." News of a new child in the family sometimes brings more worry than joy. While I discovered that many women were exuberant in their role as grandmother, I also found many others were troubled. Some felt more overburdened than overjoyed. *Will this mean my life will change? Will they want me to babysit all the time? What will I do about my job? Will they put this baby in child care eight hours a day? Are they responsible enough to handle a baby? Why, she's never even babysat, for heaven's sake!*

Sound familiar? You thought your life was starting to calm and quiet down a bit so you could do some things you'd put on hold...new drapes for the dining room, or remodeling the guest room into an office. Perhaps you even settled in with a cup of cappuccino to browse through those old travel brochures. Italy? Hong Kong? Australia? Yikes, then your daughter and her husband interrupt all your planning when they walk in beaming with news that you're going to be a grandmother. If you are fortunate enough to be reading this book before learning that you're going to be a grandparent, you can "plan" a response to the big news. That way you can enhance their joy and excitement by being supportive. No matter what you think about becoming a grandmom, we need to understand—to "get it"—that we do not have much say in the matter.

> *Excited, nervous, shocked, scared, overjoyed ... not sure!*

Some years ago, my friend Sue Girard and I had the opportunity to take a road trip to speak at a church for the weekend. Sue and I had not seen each other except to say hi and good-bye since cheering together in college more than 25 years ago. Talk about a lot of catching up to do! Our chatter made the three-hour trip fly by. Being a brand-new grandmom, I listened intently as Sue began to tell me about her beautiful four-year-old granddaughter.

It was not by her own choice that Sue had become a grandmother 4 years prior. Circumstances, to this minister family's dismay, were not ideal for their unmarried daughter, Sarah, to announce her pregnancy at 18 years old. Sarah was brought up in a household where Christian values were upheld and in a church where some in the congregation insisted that young girls get up in front of the whole church to publicly ask forgiveness if they got pregnant before marriage. Pain and confusion between this beautiful young woman, her parents, and the church culminated in the family's moving across country.

"There was no husband to hold her hand—I helped Sarah during a long, slow labor. Then, when Sarah made the decision to keep her daughter instead of going forward with adoption, I was the first to offer our home for the two of them." Though I had to keep my eyes straight ahead since I was driving, both of our eyes were brimming with tears as I reached across the front seat to hold Sue's hand.

She continued, "Since the moment I held that tiny being close to me, I've wanted nothing more than to be the best grandmother I can be for that little precious girl. I want to be a constant, positive, loving factor in her life. Her very name, Haven, comes from Psalm 107. She is an angel of blessing and restoration in Sarah's life…as well as ours. In our time of greatest distress as a ministry family, God gave us Haven, a precious treasure to us all. I tell her how beautiful she is, how thankful I am for her, and I spend as much time with her as I can. We hug and kiss a lot. I've made it my life's goal to make a difference in this little girl's life, and now for her little baby brother, as well. God is so faithful to take our mistakes and give us a ministry. God often uses Sarah these days to speak out on purity to many teen girls."

How beautiful is the love that Sue displays toward her grandchildren! I've talked to hundreds of grandmoms since then. Time after time, in conversation after conversation, I've seen a deep, loving desire in the eyes of grandmothers to devote time, resources, and love to their family members. I've seen God be faithful to that commitment. I've listened to such precious stories—no matter under what circumstances women have taken on the role as grandmother, we can all show love even when asking questions. Do any of these sound familiar?

- "I don't like being around my teen grandchildren. What can I do?"
- "My daughter and son-in-law divorced. How can I still be a good grandmother and mother to everyone involved?"
- "My son is in jail. My ex-daughter-in-law won't let me see the grandchildren. What do I do?"

- "I can't compete with the Disney World trip-giving other grandparents. I have no resources. How do I not play the comparing game?"
- "My grandson needs help. How do I convince my son that his son is self-destructing?"
- "The only time my kids let me be a grandparent is when they need a babysitter."
- "I want my grandchildren to love me and love the Lord. My kids won't even let them come over because of my Christian beliefs."

Sometimes the answer to our heart's cry can be found in that one word: *love*. That is my prayer—to be a woman of love. That is my prayer for you, as well.

I remember vividly a particular day I was feeling quite sorry for myself as I made a trip to see my grands in Missouri. I thought, *I don't get to see them often. Will I even know them? Will they even know me? I can't do for them like I see other grandmothers do. I can't take them to Disney World. I can't sew pretty ruffled dresses. I can't...*"

Yes, I was being pretty successful at self-pity. In that still moment, God impressed upon my heart, "Sharon, but you *can* love. Do you have two hands? Can you put them around a neck? Do you have a mouth? Can you speak kindness for them to hear? That's all I'm asking you to do. Just to love. Love these little ones."

The message was simple. It was loud and clear. God often shows up when I least expect Him. (After all, I think He would be the last I'd invite to a pity fest for myself!) Above all else, He was asking me simply to be a representative of Himself to my grandchildren. Just to love them. I can do that. We can do that. We can make a difference by being ourselves and loving them.

Sometimes it's the smallest things that can make the biggest difference. There's a lot we can do together. Let's change the lives and faces of grandchildren all over the world! They are our heritage. They are our history. They are our hearts. We can begin with prayer.

THE DIFFERENCE

I got up early one morning and rushed
right into the day;
I had so much to accomplish that I
didn't have time to pray.

Problems just tumbled about me and
heavier came each task.

"Why doesn't God help me?" I wondered.
He answered, "You didn't ask."

I wanted to see joy and beauty, but the
day toiled on, gray and bleak;
I wondered why God didn't show me.
He said, "But, you didn't seek."

I tried to come into God's presence;
I used all my keys at the lock.
God gently and lovingly chided,
"My child, you didn't knock."

I woke up early this morning and
paused before entering the day.
I had so much to accomplish that
I had to take time to pray.
—Grace Naessens, ca. 1960

BATHE THEM
IN PRAYER

Savoring a few last sips of tea at my breakfast table, I paused to whisper a New Year's prayer for my family as the phone rang.

"Mrs. Hoffman," the voice said. "Is your daughter home? I'm going to need some information from her regarding her being in the vehicle where the driver had been drinking last evening."

I leaned against the kitchen counter, frozen, trying to absorb the officer's words. Finally answering that my college-aged daughter was not home, I hung up the phone and reality began to set in. Feeling physically ill, I sobbed as I told my husband, Rob, about the conversation I'd just had. What a way to begin a new year! Setting aside my to-do list for the day, I was once again driven to my knees—this time in anguish. In the months that followed, we learned that what at first had seemed like a single bad decision on the part of our sweet daughter was actually part of a dangerous new lifestyle she had succumbed to at college after falling in with the wrong crowd.

During those dark days, I was to learn much about earnestly praying for a child. It was my own mother and daddy, my daughter's grandparents, who set the example, especially when I was near the point of giving up. They faithfully joined Rob and me in praying for Mindy. Her grandparents had always prayed for her and the other grandchildren, but during those tumultuous months, it was as if praying specifically for our Mindy became their solemn daily duty before God. Their prayers were a lifeline for me on days when I'd call my mother a state away and hear her say that she had just finished praying for all her grandchildren, especially for the little lamb who'd gone a-wandering.

That reassurance helped me begin to put one foot in front of the other again. I'm convinced that the greater the quality of our invisible private life spent in prayer, the more effective our visible life will be. Now, with more than ten years behind me since that tough time, I've been able to look back and see much value in those difficult months. It was then that I learned to pray as I'd never prayed before. I learned to get serious about living out this prayer:

> God, I give this child to You. I relinquish control and trust You to do whatever it takes to transform her into a person who will know You, serve You, and love You with her whole heart, soul, and mind. I don't know how and I don't know when You're going to answer, but I know I can trust You. I know You will never let her go.

Entering Our Prayer Closet

Your prayer "closet" may be your desk, a private study or guest room, or it may be under a tree or on the back porch. Some grandmoms find that some of their best prayertime is in the car. What a blessing it is and how it lifts the spirits to enter our prayer closet as the Bible calls it in Matthew 6:6 (KJV). Wherever your prayer closet may be, the important thing is to pray.

When I felt as though I had run out of ways to pray for my daughter, my mom's encouraging prayers helped me to persevere. Her cards and conversations always ended with a short promise: "I'll be praying for you every day." Constantly, I was struck with Mother's obvious consistency and never-give-up attitude of prayer. "Nana Baird," as my girls call her, was often heard to say, "I'm asking God to give Mindy a desire to return to the joy she once knew in Him." Mindy has often commented how the knowledge of a praying grandmother acted as a loving reminder for her to do right. No, my mom may not leave a vast estate when she's gone, but she will leave for me a clear example of persistent prayer, even in times of discouragement. Her eight grandchildren and six great-grandchildren have been given a lifetime of words uttered in prayer for each of them.

Your prayer "closet" may be your desk, a private study, or guest room.

God graciously and mercifully answered those prayers for the wandering one to return to the fold. The course of our family's history changed, I believe, primarily through one grandmother making prayer the most important job she would ever have. Mindy is now in her early 30s and is a godly wife, mother of three lovely daughters, and busy encouraging others to find the same sweet peace that she found years ago in her Lord. That's the legacy every grandmother on earth has a chance to leave. Prayer has an impact on future generations for eternity. As you watch your grandchildren grow up, take heart, grandmother, and know that your work, tears, and prayers are not in vain. Being the kind of grandmother that your grandkids can count on to pray for them gives them a security, knowing they are loved unconditionally.

My own mother's example of the power of prayer for such a dramatic turnaround has made a lasting impression and blessed our entire extended family. My Mindy says she is grateful for her grandmother's constant prayers. When future storms rage in Mindy's life, she knows now that the Lord's arms are around her and will sustain her, just as her grandmother's prayers have been around her, guiding her and sustaining her all these years. "What a wonderful comfort to me, knowing I have a praying grandmother. All my life I've felt her prayer and support. Every child should be so blessed!" Mindy recently exclaimed.

I take heart that my prayers for my grandchildren will be rewarded too. It's never too late to start! Think about the world in which our grandchildren live— drugs, intimidation by gang members, negative peer influences, school discipline problems, social rebellion, drunken driving, divorces, kidnappers— the list goes on. Just a look at that destructive list should infuriate us so much that we cannot stop praying. Yes, prayer works! A strong foundation of prayer for your grandchild is essential. We must bathe our grandchildren in prayer. God sees, hears, and answers.

God sees, hears, and answers.

When my grandchildren are going through something tough and my arms cannot hold them, I have discovered I must let God do the holding. When my long-distance grandchildren were here for a visit in our home, I went into the guest room where Anna and Ellie were sleeping, to kneel beside them and pray. Then, when they had traveled back to Missouri with their mom and dad, I knelt once again by the twin beds where each girl had slept, just to breathe in their sweet smell and feel close to them once again. I repeated those prayers kneeling at their bedside in our home for a week after they left. Rare were the times that tears didn't come as I prayed. At the end of that week, I finally laundered the bedding.

Yes, I'm one of those grandmoms who doesn't wash their little handprints off the glass door for about a month after they leave. I just can't bring myself to do it! I guess it makes their leaving seem so final. I know grandmoms who have long-distance grandkids understand.

PRAYER IS OUR POWERFUL, PRIMARY FUNCTION

"The primary function of grandparents," write Stephen and Janet Bly in *How to Be a Good Grandparent*, "is to pray for your grandkids." What a mighty influence we grandmoms possess when the love of a grandmother for her grandchild is connected with God's power through prayer!

Undergirded with a deep faith in God through prayer, your grandchildren will be inheriting much more from you than a pink blanket. God has given us a powerful resource with which to bring all our concerns about our loved ones to Him. Whether your grandchildren are toddlers, teens, or adults, prayer fills in any generational gap. Prayer also closes the distance gap, even if your grandchildren live hundreds of miles away. You can make a positive difference in their lives each and every day regardless of how old they are or how far away they are. You will stay connected through prayer.

I have found that by lifting my grandchildren up to God in prayer, I am drawn closer not only to them but also to Him. Prayer allows His blessings to flow to me and to those for whom I'm praying. When life is not easy and things go wrong, the prayers of spiritual grandmothers down through the ages have helped many children remember that Jesus loves them—that He is there to guide them.

The prayers of spiritual grandmothers down through the ages have helped many children remember that Jesus loves them.

With humble and tender hearts, may we grandmothers renew our spirit of commitment to God and our families through prayer. Sweet Grandma, first and foremost, can you see that it is through prayer that you and I are called to preserve the treasures that exist in our families? *"Now also when I am old and grayheaded, O God, do not forsake me until I declare Your strength to this generation, Your power to every one who is to come"* (Psalm 71:18).

With this special ministry of prayer for our loved ones comes great responsibility. We must take it seriously. Prayer will make a tremendous difference not only in years to come but even before your grandchild is born. Recently my friend Sarafaye told me about finding out that her daughter and son-in-law would have their first child after many years of praying. "The first thing I did after getting their phone call was hit my knees in thanksgiving for this gift from the Lord," Sarafaye wrote in her email. "I can't believe how much I love this grandbaby already!"

I understand. So do you. Before my last grandchild was born, I penned these words in my journal beside her sonogram picture:

> God, protect this child growing in my daughter's womb. May You hold her safely in the palm of Your protective hands. Help me to remember that when there is nothing I can do or somewhere I cannot be, You are there. There, in that dark, life-giving place, I trust Your hands.

God places great value on human life. The embryo growing inside my Mindy's body was more than just a part of her and our son-in-law Rick. It was another life—a new member of our family. God did answer this grandmother's prayers in blessing us all with baby Audrey Lane. She's such a precious gift to us.

God places great value on human life.

It was my honor to be at our other daughter Missy's side holding her hand as she and our son-in-law Mike welcomed their little Jake into this world. Right beside his sonogram in my pictorial prayer journal, I then penned and personalized the words in Psalm 139:13–16 (NIV) that David wrote thousands of years ago:

> For You created Jake's inmost being;
> You knit him together in Missy's womb.
> I praise You because Jake is fearfully and wonderfully made;
> Your works are wonderful,
> I know that full well.
> Jake's frame was not hidden from You
> When he was made in the secret place.
> When Jake was woven together in the depths of the earth,
> Your eyes saw his unformed body.
> All the days ordained for him were written in Your book
> Before one of them came to be.

I rejoice as did Hannah, "*For this child I prayed, and the* LORD *has granted me my petition which I asked of Him*" (1 Samuel 1:27).

Sweet Grandma, it may seem as if you are just one small person to this world, but *to some small person*—one grandchild—you might just *be* the world! What a big difference the loving prayers of a grandmother can make. Take the time—*make* the time—to pray. Where there's a will, there's a way.

Driving, gardening, showering, falling asleep at night, exercising...all are perfect opportunities to pray.

Driving, gardening, showering, falling asleep at night, exercising...all are perfect opportunities to pray. "Next week I've got to get organized," we tell ourselves. But I know the absolute absurdities of such a resolution. It doesn't work. It's today that is ours. The Lord knows all of today's frustrations, responsibilities, and interruptions. It's all too easy to leap into the day, and then come to the end without any prayertime, isn't it? We must define our purpose in life and intentionally make prayer an important part in our day.

Tomorrow is my 49th birthday and earlier this week I received the best birthday present I have ever received—my first grandchild. I have been so blessed in my life to experience and know many different types of love; the love of my Lord and Savior Jesus Christ, the love of my parents, my husband, my children, and now I am going to experience loving my grandchild.

As I waited for Abigail Elizabeth's arrival with a host of family and friends, I couldn't help but think how fortunate my new grandbaby was going to be. There were at least 20 people in the hospital hallway, all waiting to love her. Oh, how I wish that every baby born had a room full of people just waiting to love them!

I intend to be the best grandmother I can possibly be. I may not be able to buy her expensive toys or clothes, but I will pray for her daily and I will give her unconditional love. And one day when she is old enough to understand, I will tell her about Jesus, who loves her just as much as I do.

—Teresa Kindred, Tennessee

I once heard that we all have three ways we can look at our life: I can *waste* my life. I can *spend* my life. I can *invest* my life. Grandmoms can determine that life will be fruitful and worthwhile. We can make a difference that will last for eternity. It begins with prayer. Through our loving prayers, our grandchildren will know God's truth and love. *"One generation shall praise Your works to another, and shall declare Your mighty acts"* (Psalm 145:4).

CHOOSE TO LEAVE A LEGACY 4

We know we can become the kind of grandmothers God wants us to be because countless godly grandmothers have come before us, leading the way. We read in the Bible about Paul's spiritual son, the young preacher Timothy. I find it inspiring that early in his writing, Paul makes reference to Lois, Timothy's grandmother, and how she, along with Timothy's mom, was first to compel Timothy at a young age to strong faith in God. You and I can choose to leave this legacy too.

It is quite likely that Timothy and his mother, Eunice, may have lived with Lois in her home. How did Lois do it? She didn't have disposable diapers, precooked chicken nuggets, a microwave oven, or a superstore a block away. Something stirred her to rise above the mundane details of her life with a grace and beauty that compelled her to make a difference in the life of her grandson. When she kicked off those dusty sandals at the end of a long, hot day and unbraided her hair, I believe she continued to tune in to God's love and heavenly help.

Lois made her choice. How will we choose? If this seems like a daunting task, you're right. It is! Daunting but doable, thanks to God's promises to us. We may feel like saying to God as Moses did, "Wait a minute! Who am I that You have called me to do this job? I feel so unqualified, unskilled, unprepared, and inadequate to be a godly influence." When our confidence wanes, we can be strengthened by God's answer: *"So He said, 'I will certainly be with you'"* (Exodus 3:12).

In *Legacy of Prayer*, Jennifer Kennedy Dean has written this about her father:

My dad writes a monthly letter to friends and family. It is a collection of his observations and thoughts, newsy incidents, stories, jokes, and such. He writes on it all month long, kind of like a journal. It keeps us all in touch with each other and also provides a history. When those of us on his mailing list meet from time to time, we'll often say, 'I read about you recently in The Letter.' People share The Letter with their friends and some have even requested to be added to the mailing list. I save all the letters and they have given me many glimpses into my dad's heart. Because of The Letter, we can go back and read things such as detailed accounts of each of his grandchildren's professions of faith.

ENCOURAGEMENT FOR EVERY GRANDMOM

"I have come to realize that without Christ's help daily, raising my granddaughter would be an impossibility," says Sue, whose granddaughter lived with her the first five years of her life. As Paul says in Philippians 1:6, God will keep shaping us, perfecting us, and transforming us until we are exactly how He wants us: *"being confident of this very thing, that He who has begun a good work in you will complete it until the day of Jesus Christ."* Whew! That gives Sue and all of us some hope. So do these precious promises:

If any of you lacks wisdom, let him ask God, who gives liberally and without reproach, and it will be given to him.
—James 1:5

"Call to Me, and I will answer you and show you great and mighty things, which you do not know."
—Jeremiah 33:3

"For with God nothing will be impossible."
—Luke 1:37

"And let us not grow weary while doing good, for in due season we shall reap if we do not lose heart."
—Galatians 6:9

"Even to your old age, I am He, and even to gray hairs I will carry you! I have made, and I will bear; even I will carry, and will deliver you."
—Isaiah 46:4.

Will you join me in taking a moment to pray this prayer of dedication to be the best grandmother you can be?:

> Lord, I do want to be the best grandmother I can be. Today I'm feeling the effects of my years. On the inside, I feel as young as ever. But, outside—in my body—I need to be strengthened. I pray for the strength to forge ahead, especially that I might be a friend, an encourager, and a prayer warrior for my grandchildren. Help my life to make a difference in their lives. I ask today for strength, not only physical, but also for spiritual strength that I might be a faithful, powerful, and prayerful grandmother. I ask in Jesus's name. Amen.

LOVE ON ITS KNEES

In chapter 5, you will find Bible verses organized into topics that will help you to focus your prayers for your grandchildren. As you read, you can insert their names and make the Scriptures personal. Certainly we are to pray for their protection and that they will be caring, compassionate, and obedient children. Those character traits are among the 30 to pray, inserting their names into the Scriptures; one trait for each day of the month. But what do you do when tragedy, serious illness, or major life situations come into your grandchildren's lives?

Press on in prayer, even through sleepless nights. God is up to something.

Extensive coverage through prayer becomes our lifeline to peace during times of anguish in our families. Nothing hurts more deeply in a grandma's heart than when her grandchildren live in disobedience or practice lifestyles that seem destined to keep them far away from God. When a young person does not see the destructive path he or she is on, it sometimes is easy to get discouraged or feel tempted to give up. Is your grandchild in one of those places right now? Are you at one of those places right now? It may look as though nothing will ever change, no matter *how* much you want to pray.

Are you perhaps getting weary not seeing any answers to your prayers? From personal experience and from networking with my friends, I can confidently say this: Press on in prayer, even through sleepless nights. God is up to something. God tells us to ask and keep on asking; to seek and keep on seeking; to knock and knock loudly! (See Matthew 7:7.) God can break down a stronghold that appears impregnable. God will answer. Releasing your grandchild opens the way for God to do His work. We can trust God to continue what He has begun in our loved one's life.

BROKEN DREAMS

As children bring their broken toys
With tears for us to mend,
I brought my broken dreams to God
Because He was my friend.
But then instead of leaving Him
In peace to work alone,
I hung around and tried to help
With ways that were my own.
At last I snatched them back and cried,
"How can you be so slow?"
"My child," He said, "What could I do?
You never did let go."
—1957, author unknown, attributed to Lauretta Burns

Keep on praying. Not only for the good of your grandchild, but for yourself. I've found that my prayers change *me*. I have to first lay down my expectations and my ways of wanting God to work. I have to open my hands and let go. Isaiah 55:8 comes to my mind: *"For My thoughts are not your thoughts, nor are your ways My ways."* Often I don't grasp that verse, however, until I've exhausted myself and my ways just don't seem to be working. Releasing my grandchildren and their parents to God and letting the Holy Spirit minister to them instead of trying to step in and "fix" things is the beginning of peace in my heart.

Sometimes my most profound prayers begin with, *"Lord, I've prayed and prayed about this, and You know I'm tired of praying. I'm ready to let You have Your will in his (or her) life and not my will."* It is then that God opens the floodgates of heaven in my own heart... even if nothing at all changes in the life of the person for whom I've been praying.

The tremendous miracles of God resulting in answered prayers will eternally be a part of the legacy you leave. Your prayers make a difference; they will display God's faithfulness, sovereignty, and goodness to everyone in your family. May we grandmothers be a mighty chorus. These words from the Old Testament beautifully state our sacred charge: *"Pour out your heart like water before the face of the Lord. Lift your hands toward Him for the life of your young children"* (Lamentations 2:19).

Just as a blanket warms and keeps a grandchild secure, how much more will God's love! He wants to give our grandchildren *a future and a hope* (Jeremiah 29:11). He wants them to be confident in how very special they are to God by knowing that they are *fearfully and wonderfully made* (Psalm 139:14). God has a beautiful plan for each one of their lives. We need to fervently pray that they discover it while they are young (Jeremiah 1:5). I often remind myself of the following wise saying from Focus on the Family founder, James Dobson: "The God who made your children will hear your petitions. He has promised to do so. After all, He loves them more than you do."

Another great man of prayer, John Wesley, is frequently quoted as saying, "God will do nothing on earth except in answer to believing prayer." Who will stand in the gap for our children, schools, families, and nation if not us praying grandmothers? You are not alone in this daunting assignment—there are thousands right there in the battlefronts alongside you, on their knees as well. Satan does not want us to pray, for he knows that if the weakest saint gets on her knees, he will be defeated and not get his way in the lives of your grandchildren. Good! So let's get praying. Let's hit our "knee-mail" before we hit our email each day.

> *Who will stand in the gap for our children, schools, families, and nation?*

May each grandmom know that God will answer impossible requests, if she will but ask. Andrew Murray shared, "Persevering and believing prayer means a strong and an abundant life." William Carey stated, "Prayer—secret, fervent believing prayer, lies at the root of all personal godliness." God says,

> *"If my people who are called by My name will humble themselves, and pray, and seek My face, and turn from their wicked ways, then will I hear from heaven, and will forgive their sin and heal their land."*
> —2 Chronicles 7:14

So what does all this talk of prayer have to do with being a great grandmother? Prayer is the true enabler.

- Prayer enables us to slowly and graciously release to God what we cannot control ourselves.
- Prayer enables us to fill our hearts with compassion when we are tempted to get angry or to not forgive.

- Prayer enables us to speak the truth to a grandchild when it would be easier to pretend something didn't need to be said.
- Prayer enables us to laugh more easily with a grandchild by seeing the funny side of life.
- Prayer enables us to reconnect when time or distance is keeping us apart.
- Prayer enables the pray-er's spirit to be nourished and God's work to take place in the lives of the ones for whom prayers are lifted.

Bottom line? Prayer is *the* key to being a *great* grandmother. The investment of prayer can have resounding effects that continue for generations to come. My family today is living proof of many of my answered prayers, and God can work in all families. Now, pick up your crayons and markers, grab your creative hats, and let's get praying in some special ways for the grandmoms we'll talk about in the next chapter!

CREATE PRAYER TOOLS 5 —JOURNAL, GUIDE, AND CALENDAR

This up-close-and-personal pictorial prayer journal has been the most powerful tool I've found to equip myself to pray for my grandchildren. As well, it has been a tool for hundreds of women worldwide who have joined me to pray for children all over the world. It's my prayer that hundreds more grandmoms take time out of their busy schedules to give their grandchildren the gift of their prayers through a similar tool. You can find what works for you and adopt this idea as your own.

What grandmother does not have numerous (OK, hundreds) of pictures of her grandchildren? Over the past eight years, I've found something that helps me stay spiritually charged up in my praying. Instead of lengthy prayer lists (to me these would become long, literary endeavors that would give me panic attacks if I did not pray over each request one-by-one), I began using pictures of my family in a loose-leaf binder for my prayer prompts. I have set up a schedule and I pray for individual members of our extended family on specific days. A picture prayer journal is a working document, not a keepsake album. Make it a simple, portable, three-ring binder so the pages are replaceable as time goes by.

You won't believe how much more regularly I pray for my entire family when I use this visual format rather than long lists stuck in my Bible. The poor people at the end of my seemingly endless list rarely got more than a quick "Bless them, Lord." Another great thing is that my prayer journal is constantly changing, being updated with new photos, and I never get bored with it. Having photos of each of your family members in front of you will keep them close to your heart and remind you to pray more regularly for them.

Holding a Hand, Praying for a Heart

Each grandchild has his or her own special page and day of the week (organize yours as you like) where I take time in my morning quiet time to offer prayers specifically for that precious one. Looking at the "scrapbooked" page (I'm using that term very loosely as one who is "scrapbook challenged"), I'm focused so much better than with my old lists.

While praying, I also like to "hold their hand." I place my hand on a crayon-traced handprint of their little hands that I've glued right on their individual page. My whole family thought I was silly at first to ask for a tracing of each of their hands, but they love knowing that it was to help me pray more faithfully for them, so each obliged.

Now, there's no going back. I often take pictures of my grandchildren with the sole purpose of placing them in my prayer journal. There was the day I clicked Anna and Ellie playing in their backyard while getting along especially well, and cheerfully sharing the same riding toy. Though some days with preschoolers are exhausting, this particular moment was exhilarating.

Underneath this picture I've written: *Heavenly Father, may You protect, guide, and keep my grandchildren safe from physical harm as they play today. Lead and guide Mindy during these one-in-the-stroller-and-one-on-the-hip demanding days. Give her patience as only You can give. Let Your love shine through her today no matter what challenges she will meet. Amen.*

Alongside pictures of their little feet I've written a short prayer: *I pray that those who know (name) will say of him or her, "He or she walks with God."* Beside pictures of their hands, I've written: *Lord, bless these hands. Help them not to hit other children. May nothing these hands do or pick up from childhood to manhood or womanhood be dishonoring to You.*

From time to time, I look back through the pages that I've written in my loopy and irregular penmanship. I see so much of the faithfulness of God in my grandchildren's lives already through many answered prayers. That's an extra benefit to prayer journaling this way. I now have pages and pages of vignettes over the years that tell the recorded spiritual journey of our family. You will love retrieving these pages and remembering. I anticipate showing my grandchildren a book filled with these pages someday when they're older. They are part of my legacy to them. From these journal pages that include their lives, I pray they will understand that their grandmother learned where to go when she had nowhere to go but Jesus. I pray they will understand they were a huge part of that.

Begin today and start small. Collect some pictures of each child, and then write specific verses that apply to what is going on in each one's life right now. Insert the child's name in the verses to personalize your prayer for them. Tell your older grands that you are praying for them on a specific day and ask them for requests. Many times a grandchild will be more inclined to disclose what he or she feels they can't even share with a parent. Be a grandmother who doesn't advise—instead be one who listens and sympathizes. Then, pray.

DEVELOP SOME HOW-TO PRAYER GUIDES

"I'm praying for you. Do you have any specific requests, tests, or problems I can remember to pray about for you today?" Diana, an Iowa grandmother of seven, asks that question regularly of her grandchildren. That gives her specifics to pray about. These go in her prayer notebook. She prays expressly for each request then notes the date of answered prayer beside each request.

Let your grandchildren know you are praying for them daily.

Another grandma friend of mine, Jan, listened closely as her 11-year-old granddaughter filled her in about a friend at school who was particularly mean and constantly bullying her. This news broke Jan's heart so she asked for the child's name. Jan wanted to storm into the classroom and tell this little guy a thing or two. Instead, Jan began asking God for help with this boy in her granddaughter's class at school. Jan wasn't able to fix the problem, but she took it to God who can.

> Let your grandchildren know you are praying for them daily. Become a safe place where they may pour out their hearts, hurts, and joys. I often email or text message my grandchildren to let them know I'm specifically praying for them and that grandma loves them. All get telephone calls or hugs in person when possible, always with the message that Grandma hears, loves, cares, and constantly prays.
> —Betty Southard, grandmother extraordinaire, California

One of the most important lessons I learned from my Grams was the amount of impact a grandmother can have in the lives of her children and grandchildren. My family and I didn't realize the importance of her influence until she passed away. She taught me the importance of unconditional love through prayer, encouragements, and saying she believed in me. Sometimes a good example is the best sermon you can

have and I had this from my Grams. She has left a legacy of prayer and it will continue to live on through me.
—Melissa, age 31

The message from Melissa is pretty clear—praying for our grandchildren *is* noted in their lives, and it *does* make a difference.

DEVELOP A MONTHLY PRAYER CALENDAR

To get you started, here is a list of 30 godly goals and virtues grandmoms might ask God to develop in their grandchildren's lives. You can pick one trait per week for concentrated prayer, or another option would be to pray for each of traits consistently one day each month, which would give you the opportunity to pray this entire list 12 times in a year. A month of character qualities for current and future needs could include these, and you may think of additional ones to add:

1. **Joy**—Psalm 97:11; 16:11; Isaiah 55:12; Philippians 4:4
2. **Patience**—Psalm 40:1; Hebrews 10:35–36; Hebrews 12:1; James 1:3, 4
3. **Salvation**—Psalm 34:10; Matthew 6:33; Luke 12:31; 2 Timothy 3:15
4. **Friends**—Proverbs 1:10–11; Romans 12:2; Ephesians 4:32; 1 Peter 3:8
5. **Respectfulness toward parents**—Exodus 20:12; Deuteronomy 5:16; Proverbs 23:22; Ephesians 6:2; Titus 3:1
6. **Control of the tongue**—Psalm 19:14; Proverbs 11:13; James 3:1–12
7. **Fearlessness**—Psalm 16; 23; 91; 2 Corinthians 12:9
8. **Unselfishness**—Isaiah 41:10; Nehemiah 8:10; Colossians 3:12; 1 Peter 5:5
9. **Finding God's will**—Psalm 40:8; 37:4; Proverbs 3:5, 6
10. **Total dedication to God**—Mark 12:20; Romans 6:23; 8:29; Galatians 5:22
11. **Forgiveness**—Matthew 18:22–35; Ephesians 4:32; 1 John 1:9
12. **Peace**—Psalm 29:11; Isaiah 26:3; Colossians 3:2
13. **Healing from illness**—Psalm 32:18; 2 Thessalonians 2:16, 17; 1 Peter 2:24
14. **Faith and confidence in times of trouble**—Psalm 46:1–2; Deuteronomy 31:8; Matthew 6:26; Philippians 4:13
15. **Freedom from jealousy**—Proverbs 6:34; 26:27; Galatians 5:26
16. **Dependability**—Psalm 90:17; Proverbs 16:3; 1 Corinthians 9:23–27
17. **Protection from the evil one**—Luke 21:31; John 17:15
18. **Obedience**—Genesis 18:19; Psalm 32:6
19. **Kindness**—Psalm 139:23, 24; Ephesians 4:32; James 1:19
20. **Purity**—Romans 1:1–20; 1 Corinthians 6:18–20; 13:4–5; Titus 3:5

21. **Submissiveness to God**—Matthew 6:33; Romans 8:29; James 4:7; 1 Peter 3:1–7
22. **Hatred for sin**—Psalm 97:10; Matthew 26:41
23. **Courage**—Deuteronomy 31:6; Psalm 34:4, 8, 18; 56:3, 4, 8
24. **Self-discipline**—Proverbs 13:4; 20:13
25. **Passion for God**—1 Chronicles 29:18; Psalm 63:8
26. **Responsibility**—Galatians 6:5; Hebrews 12:1
27. **Gratefulness**—Ephesians 5:20; Philippians 4:12–13; Colossians 2:7
28. **Self-acceptance**—Psalm 139; Ephesians 1:6
29. **Comfort when brokenhearted**—Psalm 147:3, 5; 2 Corinthians 1:4–5
30. **Desire to be a testimony**—Matthew 5:14–16

Heavenly Father, You have abundantly blessed me with grandchildren. Thank You for their precious lives. Help me to be a blessing to them. Although I'm thankful for the material possessions You've given me, I'm most grateful for my family— the blessings I can take to heaven with me. I pray for my grandchildren. I want to be there in the events of their lives, I want to be there with hugs when they are hurting, lonesome, or fearful. May I be reminded that the most effective thing I can do is pray for them. Teach me to be quiet and listen for Your will and Your response. Amen.

30 godly goals and virtues

Write your own special prayer for your little angels and/or older grandchildren here:

_____

_____

_____

_____

_____

_____

_____

_____

_____

_____

Of all the many opportunities and blessings I have had in my life, being the wife, mother, and now grandmother of such a loving family is my most cherished role. Join me as we venture into some ways to make grandmothering fun as we live, laugh, and love our grands in style.

BLESSED ARE THE GRANDMOMS WHO MAKE TIME

6

When I began to ask for responses from grandmothers at women's conferences, I was totally unprepared for what one grandmother stopped me in the hall to say to me. "The term *grandmother* sounds so old and frumpy to me. This is *my* time," she began. "I've done my stint and those children belong to my kids. If they didn't want to take care of them, they shouldn't have had them. Let them take care of their own kids. I've done my time. I want to do *my* thing while I still can!"

I wondered what I'd gotten myself into.

I was so taken aback that it took a bit for me to realize she wasn't teasing me. I thought a few moments, and then replied in my sweetest voice possible, "Oh, what a privilege you're missing out on! I'm so glad to be young enough to have fun with my grandchildren, pray for them, and teach them about the love of God. It doesn't make me feel old to carry their pictures in my wallet. I whip them out any chance I get."

Dumbfounded, she didn't say a word, so I went on to say something like, "My heart skips a beat when I hear my grands running up the walk calling out, 'Nana, Nana,' while I hide and pop out at them. I admit to looking around for headache medicine after some visits, but I feel I'm living right now in the best season of my life. I wouldn't want to miss out on the joy of grandchildren for anything. In fact, they make me feel young again. I'm so grateful for every day and for the memories we're making together."

I don't think that was the answer this woman expected or wanted to hear. She then proceeded to give various reasons to substantiate her current disdain of grandmothering—much of which was based on her brand-new white carpeting and the hours required to complete a rigorous daily gym routine. (Hmmm, I do recall she was wearing spandex).

Maybe you can identify. I've learned so much from women during my years of speaking and ministering to them. Women everywhere voice this struggle of finding balance. But, ladies, while you have much on your to-do list, you have so much to offer a grandchild! Your experience and insights make you the perfect guide for helping a grandchild successfully navigate the sometimes turbulent waters of day-to-day living.

It used to be that a grandmom always had time for the grandkids. Their lives were at a slower pace that seemed to be the perfect complement for busy youngsters. But now, maybe it's because grandmoms are younger, or we have more things that we can do, grandmothers don't seem to be as accessible as they used to be. I guess that's why I'm convinced deep in my soul that the presence of an unselfish, godly grandmom is more indispensable than ever.

> I used to think that *Grandmother* meant 'old.' But, when I became one I discovered quite the opposite. Grandmother, or Mimi, as my title goes, opens up the wonderful, magical world of seeing life once again through a child's eyes. That makes me feel young.
> —Rebecca Barlow Jordan, a Texas grandmom

May God make us faithful grandmothers realize our holy responsibility before Him to encourage our young ones in their talents, schoolwork, character, faith, and in every way we possibly can toward heaven. So much more important than what we place in our grandkids' hands is what we place in our grandkids' hearts. The gifts we place in our grandchildren's hearts will never wear out, lose value, or go out of style.

LIFE HAPPENS WHILE WE MAKE OTHER PLANS

Showing love is more valuable than anything a million dollars could buy. My heart grieves for children in this generation who are missing out by not being able to spend extended time with their grandparents. Not to imply that doing so is always easy. I realize there are often health, employment, and distance restrictions, but may I say emphatically that the love of a grandmother is a most valued gift!

You don't have to go to grandmothering school to learn what to do. Noted authority on the family James Dobson put it so well when he said recently on his radio program, *Focus on the Family,* "To a child, love is spelled 'T-I-M-E.'"

I suppose I first was truly awakened to this truth when spending nights as a young girl with my Grandma Alta. My daddy married my mother two years after my birth mother's death, and I have never forgotten the gentle acceptance that my "new" grandmother showed me. I was a lonely, frightened, rather spirited (nice way to say *bratty*) little girl. She made me feel special as only a grandmother could. The hours she gave for me and the time she spent with me are as many as the stars in the sky.

Most of all, Grandma Alta made me feel special being *me*. She didn't have to accept me as one of her grandchildren. After all, I wasn't a true relative, not by blood. But, she did accept me. That unconditional loving acceptance remains to this day an invisible reminder of the power of a grandmother's love. Simple gestures such as buying me a fluffy purple dress for Christmas one year that was identical to my cousin's spoke volumes. That gift signified that I was included in the brood of grandchildren—my dress was the same as theirs. To a little eight-year-old girl struggling daily with self-acceptance, that was huge. The message: *Sharon, you are accepted!*

Ah, and there were those sleepovers. I loved getting to stay all night at Grandma Alta's. I'd try my best to lie really still at night so she would be able to fall asleep with me close beside her. Then wide-eyed, I'd lie silently watching the curtains gently blowing in the summer night's breeze and review all the fun things we'd done together that day. Berry picking, rolling our hair on pink sponge rollers, walking to the grocery (something Alta did every single day), sitting on the porch discussing the flowers blooming in her garden while sniffing pleasant honeysuckle on the fence... I have a lifetime of joys with Grandma Alta to look back and reflect upon. Such gifts she gave me! Not expensive in terms of this world, but priceless to me.

I value you enough to spend time with you.

Here's the message those grandma gifts conveyed to me: *"I value you enough to spend time with you."* No matter how busy or how involved she may have been in a project, Grandma Alta considered me more important. She gave me her full, undivided attention the times when I went over to spend the night. That meant a lot. She knew I liked mashed potatoes and sliced tomatoes, so if she had the slightest notion that I'd be over for dinner, that's what she'd have. I loved that about her and did not realize how important she was in my life until I became a grandmother. Now, if I think grandkids are going to be over for a mealtime—yes, you guessed it—I do the same thing.

YOU DON'T HAVE TO BE PERFECT, JUST PREPARED

My Grandma Alta is in heaven now, but the memory of sweet times with her can still bring tears to my eyes. She wasn't perfect. I'm sure she'd say, "Far from it." Real grandma love strengthens and helps grandchildren mature securely. To do that takes sacrifice and the setting aside of our own plans sometimes. Yes, unselfishness is required. The cost is often pricey. But, we must ask ourselves, what will be the cost of *not* making this God-given role a priority?

Most grandmoms I know would not dare tell anyone or give any indication that they think grandchildren are a burden and a problem. No one actually says *that*. Ladies, there are times when life schedules and demands take control of all of us if we let them. An inventory of our daily calendar in this season in life may be long overdue. We must firmly establish in our own hearts what in life we need to hold on to and what we can let go of.

> *We must firmly establish in our own hearts what in life we need to hold on to and what we can let go of.*

How does so much busyness creep into our lives? We make the mistake of thinking that busyness makes us look important. Or that busyness is good or godly. To counteract busyness we must make time for quiet, solitude, and restoration. Making time for the Lord and being in His Word is essential if we are to hear from God about the direction of our lives.

If we are to busy to be with the God of the Universe—the Lord of our lives—we are too busy.
—Donna Otto, *The Gentle Art of Mentoring*

My prayer is that even those with doubts will see that though grandmothering may be our most challenging journey, it can be our most rewarding. What could be more rewarding than letting a child know he or she is special? God thinks our grands are very special, and we must not ever forget that He thinks we are very special too:

> *For You formed my inward parts;*
> *You covered me in my mother's womb.*
> *I will praise You, for I am fearfully and wonderfully made,*
> *Marvelous are Your works,*
> *And that my soul knows very well.*
> —Psalm 139:13, 14

I encourage us all to cut out or slow down in one area of our lives this week. Bottom line? We all have time to do what we want to do. We seem to find time if we're interested in something or somebody. Ask God every day to allow you to see areas where you might be willing to rearrange your life to make it less busy and more available or accessible to the loved ones in your life. Additionally, let Him show you when you are caught up in hurry, hurry, hurry.

> When you help someone up a mountain, you'll find yourself close to the summit too.
> —Author Unknown

DON'T JUST SAY IT—PRAY IT!

Let's face it. We all battle the "selfishness thing." Not thrilled about having grandchildren in your life? Clearly, that may be the number-one thing that grandmoms just don't talk about. If you are nodding your head, agreeing that you've felt that way at times; take comfort—you are not alone. Though few would dare to say aloud, *Boy, I wish I didn't have grandchildren*, many have thought it.

A long time ago, I heard a speaker say, "The best way to combat selfishness is to cultivate thankfulness." When I find myself "growling" and having an ugly, selfish attitude, that's when God seems to prompt me to pray a prayer of recommitment and renewal to Him, a promise to do His will; not to have my way. I do long to love my grandchildren as deeply as the generations of grandmoms who have faithfully preceded me. But I cannot do it in my own strength.

Neither can you. Would you agree? Some grandmoms are facing pretty tough battles. I know that you are—I've spoken with you and heard your stories. To get you on your way, consider the following prayer as a guide to help bring back the joy in your role of grandmothering, as well as reestablish priorities. God specializes in makeovers. Join me, won't you, as I pray the following again today:

> Lord God, my heavenly Father, thank You that You can heal and thank You that it is never too late. Help me to be grateful for and worthy of the important role of being a grandmother.
>
> Sometimes I feel trapped. Burdened. Guilty. At times I wish I could just go away and be somebody else for a while. Maybe the young girl I used to be...or maybe the woman I've not even yet become.
>
> Lord, it's hard to balance all that needs my time and attention. My work, house, husband, friends, children, and grandchildren—I feel so burdened by it all. Show me Your priorities. Help me to be conscious of You beside me. It's all too much—please help me know Your peace.

Make me wise in all I do and say (or not say). Help me to know that grandparenthood is a part of the purpose You've ordained for my life.

Help me as I choose to obey You in these times. I offer my life, my heart, and when needed, my home. Give me a godly grandmother's heart.

I wish, my Father, that I could reach out and touch each one of my children and grandchildren today. I know in my heart of hearts, that my arms are not long enough. My lap is not big enough.

Yet I know that You are big enough. Reach them for me. Keep them safe in the shelter of Your love. I need forgiveness for when I fail the little ones You have put into my keeping. I put my will, my life, my desires, my ambitions, my children and grandchildren into Your hands.

How they need You in these times, Lord.

How I, their grandmother, need You too.

Stand close by me as I stand for them. Amen.

Therefore encourage one another and build each other up, just as in fact you are doing.
—1 Thessalonians 5:11 (NIV)

ENCOURAGE EFFECTIVELY

7

No, we don't have to be perfect as grandmothers. We're never going to be perfect, but we can be prepared. The day will come when you—yes, *you*—might be the only one who is your grandchild's encourager. We all need to be prepared for that day. The following sweet story best illustrates what I'm saying.

One day a grandmother noticed something under a big oak tree while playing in the park with her grandson. She watched as a line of children began to form. Under the tree was an artist painting pictures on the darling, wide-eyed faces of the children. One by one they would scamper away joyously thrilled with their butterfly, heart, or flower colorfully painted on their cheeks.

The grandmom nodded to her grandson, indicating that he could run over to have his face painted. She sat down on a nearby park bench to watch. It wasn't but a few seconds before her little guy ran back over to where she was sitting. He was sad-faced with tears streaming down his face.

She was shocked. "Why, what's the matter?"

"Sh-sh-she said," the grandson managed to begin between sobs, "She said I couldn't have my face painted because there are too many freckles on it."

Wisely, this dear grandmom cupped her grandson's cheeks in both of her hands and lifted his tear-stained, little face. "Why, I can't think of *anything more beautiful* than freckles," she answered quietly.

"I can," came his reply. "Wrinkles."

How I love the grandmom in that story! She loved on her grandson and elevated his self-respect. One can never evaluate how quickly a person's feelings of self-worth depreciate after a remark or an attitude that is unkind. It can take the wind right out of a child's sails and leave him deflated. When we contribute to someone's personal worth, we build them up and they will love you for it. As a side note, I want to say that I imagine that strong grandmom then marched right over to the artist's umbrella and her grandson promptly got his face painted!

If you're feeling depressed, overwhelmed, or cheated, you're most likely focusing on what you *don't* have. You can grow gratitude by recognizing blessings you *do* have, no matter how insignificant they seem. You'll see life in a different way and may find yourself going down a different path.
—Deborah Norville, *Today's Christian Woman*

KNOW THE POWER OF A POSITIVE WORD

The grandson in that story got the message. It couldn't have been more loud and clear. "I love you. You are precious to me just the way you are." Call his grandmother a stubborn, feisty grandmom; I call her one who knows how to show love with her words. The next time you are with one of your grandchildren, no matter what their age, build them up. When they tell a joke, you be the one who laughs the loudest. Showing appreciation and pleasure at their creative accomplishments provides supportive self-confidence. Encourage your grandchildren toward the activities for which they seem to have an aptitude (sports, music, art, drama, and so on). Praise decisions of older grandchildren that are moral and wholesome, and those that help them reach their special goals and dreams.

Examine and observe each of your grandchildren, noting these special qualities and aptitudes.

Each child is born with certain abilities and gifts to offer to the world. Examine and observe each of your grandchildren, noting these special qualities and aptitudes. Ask God to help you understand how they can be developed and used. Share with them the potential you see in them. None of them is exactly like anyone else—not their parents, not you, not your other grandchildren. We may see similarities in temperament and appearance, but each is unique with incredible possibilities.

Thus, our challenge is to not compare. Nothing will make a child (or his parents) shut down quicker. Our task is to encourage, not discourage. Allow each one to do his or her best and to grow and develop at each child's God-given pace. Support all their endeavors and allow God to work in their lives as they test out different directions. God may have a whole different plan for their life than you might think He does.

There is only one God—and it is not me, nor you. He knows what's best, better than we do. It would do us good to remember that. Case in point: Joni Eareckson Tada. She was a wonderfully active teenager who loved swimming and had high hopes for the future. But God had other plans for her. A diving accident paralyzed her just below the neck at age 17. Joni had to adjust her life and goals accordingly. Her parents and grandparents were required to do the same in healthy and affirming ways. I'm sure that wasn't easy. After reading several of her books and meeting her in person, I can bear witness that today Joni is a wonderfully accomplished artist, singer, and author who is an inspiration to everyone everywhere she goes.

We don't know what the future holds. We're just called on to keep our eyes fixed on Jesus. We can hold on to the assurance that God is at work in our grandchildren's lives and in ours. He knows, better than we do, the "rest of the story." He's working all things *to will and to do for his good pleasure* (Philippians 2:13). Ask the Father to help you even in simple ways to become your grandchild's biggest cheerleader.

> The happiness of life is made up of minute factors—the little soon-forgotten charities of a kiss or smile, a kind look, and a heartfelt compliment.
> —Samuel Taylor Coleridge

DUST OFF YOUR CHEERLEADING POM-POMS

Let's stop and think right now. What seeds are you sowing in the hearts of your grandchildren? Positive or negative? Are we planting kind and gracious words that will produce positive responses in the fertile grounds of their minds? We do reap what we sow—let us not grow weary while doing good for those we love. Ask the Holy Spirit to show you areas where you might need to change the seed you're sowing so you will reap bountifully. Ask God to remove any preconceived ideas of how He is going to use your grandchildren for His glory. Never limit God by presuming to take His work upon yourself.

> *"For My thoughts are not your thoughts,*
> *Nor are your ways My ways," says the LORD.*
> *"For as the heavens are higher than the earth,*
> *So are My ways higher than your ways,*
> *And My thoughts than your thoughts."*
> —Isaiah 55:8–9

I believe one of the greatest needs in our day is encouragement.
—Bill Wellons, in *The Power of an Encouraging Word* by Ken Sutterfield

We should ask the Lord to give us a fresh revelation of ways we can be our grandchild's cheerleader. Each day, we must ask ourselves, *How can I be an encouragement today?* Do what you can, when you can, where you can, however you can. Write a note or email. Make a phone call. It doesn't hurt to prepare with a good word or two on your mind. We must *prepare*, so we don't have to *repair* later. Here are some words that can jump-start our plans to cheer on our grandchildren:

- Terrific!
- Keep up the good work.
- You made that look so easy.
- Great job!
- You did it!
- You've got it!
- Now that was good work.
- What a good listener.
- You mean so much to me.
- How did you make that?
- You just made my day!
- Exceptional performance today.
- I've never known anyone your age to do that!
- I like your smile.
- Great job!
- Keep working on it—I just know you can do it!
- You're the best!
- Way to go!
- You are absolutely beautiful.
- Now that's a good piece of art.
- You are a darling.
- No princess was ever more lovely!
- I like the way you work.
- You're getting better at it all the time!
- Our family wouldn't be the same without you.
- You light up my home when you come over!
- A-OK!
- You're right.

- I sure do love you.
- I'm so proud of you!
- Picking up your toys was so responsible of you!
- I like it when you do the dishes with me. You're so helpful.
- You didn't give up! You dressed all by yourself!
- What a hard worker you are!
- I love you more than chocolate chip ice cream.

Grandmas are moms with lots of frosting.
—Anonymous

KNOW THAT YOU HAVE A LOT TO OFFER

We should spend our lives perfecting our capacity to honor and compliment others. Personal relations are vitally important to successful, joyful living. Use what you have and who you are to build up, not tear down others. That's a much better way to live—infinitely better than belittling people, including our grandchildren's parents. (We will address this subject further in Chapter 12.)

While writing this chapter, I'm reminded how precious a good word can be. I remember an event in which my mentor (a grandmother in the faith) gave me the powerful gift of positive words. Enjoying a conference luncheon with Norma Gillming, English professor and public speaker extraordinaire, I did not yet know how much this great woman's words would later mean to me.

I had no way of knowing that she would be introducing me right before I got up to speak to the auditorium full of women later that evening. Instead of turning her comments to the audience, Mrs. G. began addressing me personally as she stood at the podium holding a long-stemmed, gold-dipped rose. "I have always liked you, Sharon. I believe in you. I knew when I first met you; you were a freshman in college. I knew then that you had great possibilities. I am so very, very proud of you."

She went on to say some affirming words about me and about my ministry. Words I shall never forget. They ring in my ears to this day. As I remember walking onto the platform to speak through a mist of tears, I realize that I have never forgotten what Mrs. G. said or how she said it. That, my dear friend, is the power of a woman's words.

Grandmothers, we can make a big difference in our grandchildren's lives... and those children will go on to make a huge difference in this world. Be a grandmom for God! I hope you're confident that no one can have a greater impact on the extended family than you as a grandma.

Some day we'll meet Jesus in the air… *"and so we will be with the Lord forever"* (1 Thessalonians 4:17 NIV). How wonderful knowing that our final destination is a glorious home where we'll live forever with Him! No deadlines to meet, no diapers to change, no cellulite, no sagging, no weariness, no busyness nor impending stress. Our heavenly Father will welcome us with open arms to a place beyond the reaches of our imagination. I can hardly wait!

We can all serve the Lord in caring for our grandchildren through the so-called little things.

Dearest grandmom, in that day we'll find that every hug we've hugged, every prayer we've prayed, every bedtime story we've read, every tear we've kissed away, every encouraging word we've spoken, every promise we've kept truly mattered. Continue to give of your heart and of yourself. Let God's love spill out from you onto the lives of your grandchildren. Put your arm around that dear, treasured grandson or granddaughter and say, "I am so glad you are mine."

If you are the primary caregiver of your grandchildren, I'm sure that sometimes you (like all of us, if we're honest) lose perspective of the high calling God has given you to diligently raise those children He has loaned to your keeping. Sometimes the mundane routines and the constant demand to meet needs can become either overwhelming or discouraging. Maybe you feel like one friend of mine who said, "There's got to be more to this than there seems."

That's where God's Word steps in to remind us of what is important. We can all serve the Lord in caring for our grandchildren through the so-called little things like wiping runny noses, making meals, washing clothes, and other everyday duties. I feel as though Jesus also was talking directly to weary grandmoms when He said these words:

> *"For I was hungry and you gave Me food; I was thirsty and you gave me drink; I was a stranger and you took me in. . . . Assuredly, I say unto you, inasmuch as you did it to one of the least of these . . . you did it to Me."*
> —Matthew 25:35, 40

Jesus's promise is so liberating! He tells us that even when we give a cup of water (or fruit drink) that we are fulfilling a God-given responsibility. Even when the world does not place very high honor on raising young ones in the Lord, let us remember Jesus's words. What we do for our grandchildren, we do for Jesus. Let's keep that perspective—even a simple cup of cold water can be ministry to our grandchildren and an act of worship to our great God. Let's keep filling those sippy cups. While we're at it, let's say a positive word of kindness to let the love of God overflow from His heart into the hearts of our grandchildren.

Your grandchild, like all of us, desperately needs your affirming blessing that he is wanted and loved by you, and is not an interruption in your busy life. He may have almost given up on ever being loved—really loved. In despair, as he gets older, he may begin to try to fill the hole in his heart with sex, violence, wild friends, bullying, drugs, or alcohol. Those actions are attempts to block his sadness and pain. We must take time to think, pray, and consider how God can shape our attitudes and actions so that we will become a more positive factor in our grandchild's life.

Let God make you over! Be willing to let God help you more effectively communicate unselfish love and a positive influence. Apart from Him, you and I are incapable of loving. Be willing to be like Jesus, who gave and gave and kept on giving. In essence, His love is the absence of self. No judging. No searching for wrong motives. No self-righteousness. Just a proactive extension of the grace that flows to us from the Father's heart. Let your grandchild rest securely in that love, clearly lighting the way to the Savior. You will be changing lives for many years to come.

Join me in the next chapter as we meet more grandmoms who are stepping out and stepping up to meet the challenges of grandmothering in fun-loving, laugh-out-loud ways.

Be Remembered as a Fun, Gutsy, Grandmom

8

Smiling, laughing, having fun ... those are the memories we want our grandchildren to hold of us in their hearts. We certainly don't want a picture of a grumpy, grouchy grandma. Let your laughter ring in their ears after visits together.

In a world where children today are involved in so many more activities than anyone would ever imagine, fun often doesn't just happen spontaneously. Sometimes you have to plan it.

A few years ago, my granddaughter Ellie and I were passing the time on a family trip by playing one of our favorite road games, "I spy." It was Ellie's turn and she had me searching high and low for something purple, our favorite color. It wasn't the beach towel, the flower on her shirt, or her purple nail polish. I had a good view of the entire van from my backseat location, but it wasn't helping. What else could it possibly be?

"You'll never guess this one," the seven-year-old announced. That was all I needed to hear. Zooming down the highway at 70 miles per hour, my competitive streak went into overdrive.

But there was nothing purple left in the car. "Are you sure you mean purple?" I asked, eying her sister Christina and the sweater she wore, "Could it be pink?"

"No, Nana, it's purple. I promise." She crossed her arms. "You might as well give up. You'll never guess."

Five minutes later, I gave up. "OK, what is it?"

She pointed. I leaned over and scanned the floorboard. "There's nothing purple down there."

"Not there. There," she said pointing again.

I followed her pointing finger straight to my left. My spider-veined leg.

Purple is no longer my favorite color.

—Vonda Skelton, South Carolina

To help get those creative juices flowing, the ideas in this chapter come from a wonderful network of fun grandmoms from far and wide and show us how to "let loose" and have a blast with our darlings, whether tots or teens. Included in this chapter are ideas for

- establishing or renewing a fun-filled home;
- thinking and playing "out of the box";
- celebrating special occasions and holidays;
- teaching grandchildren games that kids won't learn from anyone but grandparents;
- establishing fun five-minute breaks for little ones and kids of all ages;
- using play to teach; and
- expanding your vision for fun.

Don't Be Afraid to Have Fun

It pays to use your imagination, ingenuity, and sense of humor when making memories with your grandchildren. That means memories of lots of "get-down-on-the-floor" play. It doesn't matter if it is a structured game or impromptu roughhousing on the floor. In play, kids can be whatever they want to be. They can be Michael Jordan in the front driveway shooting hoops, explorers for ancient treasure in the woods behind your house, bakers and/or dump truck operators in the sandbox...the whole world is a child's playground. We must never discourage good, healthy, appropriate play. We need to encourage it—and join in.

The presence of a grandparent confirms that parents were, indeed, little once, too, and that people who are little can grow to be big, can become parents, and one day even have grandchildren of their own. So often we think of grandparents as belonging to the past; but in this important way, grandparents, for young children, belong to the future.

—Fred Rogers, quoted by Willard Scott

Play gives kids some exercise and allows them to use up some of their seemingly endless supply of energy. (That's especially important to remember when grandchildren are staying at our house for a summer, a week, or even overnight.)

When was the last time you sharpened your physical skills by getting down and dirty in play with your grandchild? Being an adult doesn't mean that you're not to play anymore. We're allowed. We're encouraged to—even if we feel we're starting from scratch.

When I conducted interviews with dozens of grandchildren of all ages, I heard over and over, "My grandmother is fun! I remember she always played with us" or "I remember vacations at my Grammy's house when we'd play such-and-such." The name of the game varied, but the idea was the same. Their Grandmas liked to play with them!

So, let's play on!

Scoot your family room furniture up against the walls and play some tumbling games with your small grandchildren. Dig out that old blanket and set up a tent using two kitchen chairs. Race your youngster to the garage, don helmets, and have a bike ride together pretending to be a naturalist in search of a rare tiger in your neighborhood. Grab your son's baseball mitt and throw softballs with your grandsons. Oh, how they'll get a kick out of you! The joys you'll feel and smiles you'll see on your grands' faces will more than make up for the occasional mess or two.

Don't let go of your playfulness.

Plus, for us teachers at heart, I remind us all that blending the world of play and pretend has long been one of the best teaching tools ever. How great to see a child learning something while having a ball doing it! While on that "expedition" we can be teaching knowledge, wisdom, and experience right along with the fun of playing.

We've got the power to do just that. Everything we need is either right under our nose or quite easily accessible. Use imagination to come up with new and creative ways to create a playful climate right at home (theirs if you are child-sitting). We can bring fun into any room and into any day.

It may take a conscious effort on our part at first, especially if getting down and dirty is not our style. Don't let go of your playfulness just because you're all grown up. Revive silliness! Loosen up! Learn some jokes. My mother is 80 years old; kids of all ages love her and comment about how fun it is to be with her. (She taught second grade in school in the same classroom for almost 30 years.) Now even the great-grandchildren look forward to going places with her or to her house. Who was the one having the most fun last fall on the hayride exploring a nearby farm? Yes, you're right. Great-Grandma Lindy. She made the day more fun for everybody. Someone said, "Grandmother-grandchild relationships are simple. Grandmas are short on criticism and long on love."

Study to be a fun grandmother if you need to do so. Be a student of play. Watch young children playing. Learn how to play the games and sports your grandchildren are into. Ask questions about their sport, and have them teach you what it is they are learning. And you don't have to always grasp the concepts too quickly. Ask lots of questions so that they will have to continue instructing you. That shows that you are truly interested in them and what they are into.

"So," you might say casually, "tell me, how you did you get so good at swinging a bat? I'd like to try if you'll show me how." You'll have a beaming grandchild whose self-worth just went up several notches. They enjoy being the teacher, especially if the student is their grandmom.

> Play is a child's work and toys are the tools....Different kinds of play can foster different skills, such as language, gross and fine motor movements, and imagination.
> —Dr. T. Berry Brazelton, pediatrician, author,
> and former host of *What Every Baby Knows*, quoted by Willard Scott

Praise your grands for good sportsmanship and instruct them to be good losers. Better than that, *show* them how to be a good loser by your example when you play games together. Remember, they are taught by what you do much more than what you say.

Be on the lookout for those things that have the potential for being played together. Don't be afraid to try something new, even if it's a little weird or awkward to you at first. You'll be so glad you did. It may just become your grandchild's favorite memory that sticks in his mind forever.

> Grandmother—a wonderful mother with lots of practice.
> —Author Unknown

CREATE MEMORIES OF FUN RITUALS AND GAMES

As you learn to play more with your grandchildren, you will find yourself creating more of a playful, fun climate in your home. It takes practice, but you can do it. One grandma, Sandie, made a "train" out of six dining room chairs one rainy afternoon when she had her five grandchildren for the day. She'd hoped to take them swimming, but a sudden thunderstorm prevented them from going.

"They had so much fun sounding the whistle, getting off and on at various 'train stops' and taking turns being the conductor. Now, any time the grandchildren are over, even without their cousins there, they always burst through the door saying, 'Where do we get our ticket for the train ride today, Grams?'"

Ah, yes. What she thought would be just a rainy-day diversion turned into one of the most fun rituals now at Grandma Sandie's house. My guess is that those children will have priceless stories to tell when they are older about riding the train at Grams. What fun!

> My Great-grandmother, which is what we had to call her (no cute nicknames for her!), knew how to have fun. She once told me that the reason she sings hymns when she washes dishes is that it makes the chore fun and go by faster. To this day when I do the dishes, I sing hymns and praise songs; it really does work.
> —Joann Spain, a grandmother in Ohio

REMIND YOURSELF THAT WHERE THERE'S IMAGINATION, THERE'S A WAY

Being a long-distance grandmom to three of my grands, I wanted the five days when they all came rolling in last year at Thanksgiving, needless to say, to be fun, yet not too full of frenzy. The last thing I wanted was for this Nana's house to be borrrr-ring.

By the third day, I'd exhausted all the tricks up my sleeve and needed a fresh supply of adventures for the five grands to do together. Spotting a huge box in our garage (leftover from a new recliner that had been delivered.), I asked my husband, Rob, to bring it into the house. Guess what? It was *the* hit of the visit!

A cardboard box still has the power to serve a vital function.

Small children have active imaginations, so I played off of that. We formed a line and crawled through our new "tunnel." We became different animals with identifying sounds. We carried in stuffed animals, and the box turned into a zoo. We dressed up in silly borrowed dress-up clothes and became princesses having tea in our super-duper living-room-sized "castle" with our "prince"—a good way to involve the only one of our grandchildren who is a boy! Probably the highlight was when Poppa Rob became a monster attacking the castle by banging the outside of the box while we all giggled inside. "Fee, fie, foe, fum..." You should have heard them squeal! Of course, the more they screamed, the more Grandpa Rob played.

I was thoroughly delighted to find out that a cardboard box still has the power to serve a vital function even in this twenty-first-century techno world. All the children gravitated to the box off and on those last two days of their visit. Finally, we even used it as a makeshift snow sled when our hill out back got a dusting of snow. We got enough good out of that box to justify the cost of our new recliner!

Try out these additional possibilities for pretend play that appeal to younger age groups:

- Blanket Fort—Never underestimate the power of this tried-and-true, longtime favorite of kids. Drape your dining table with several sheets. Tape posters or stars to the bottom of your table, then lie on the floor looking up at them together. Kids of all ages love blanket forts—you can vary the play according to their interests or a current book they are reading.
- Goin' Fishin'—Make a big "fish pond" with a blue bath rug. Have the kids draw fish on heavy construction paper, cut them out, and glue or tape paper clips to them. Make "fishing poles" from sticks with string and refrigerator magnets taped to the ends. Scatter the fish on the rug and "go fishing." See who can catch the most fish before the timer goes off at five minutes. (Watch carefully if small children are playing with small paper clips or magnets that they could swallow or get lodged in an ear or a nostril.)
- Goofy Picnic—Spread out a big blanket in an unlikely place to have a picnic (such as your attic, basement, or the back of your truck). Get snack yummies for your picnic, or have a full-fledged sandwiches-and-chips lunch. Be sure to get some plastic ants and flies to have handy in your pocket. The kids will love it when they start appearing on the blanket or their food. Serve cupcakes decorated with cute little ladybugs or gummy worms.
- The Vacuum Is Loose!—Invent a story about the "vacuum animal" having escaped from the zoo. It's now roaming through your house. From screaming and running to get on "base," to creating more to the story themselves, kids love this. Wait till you hear their squeals of delight even over the sound of the vacuum (which you are pushing around).

- Treasure Hunt—Organize a treasure hunt indoors or outdoors. Make it simple for young children by hiding big objects in easy-to-spot places. Stuffed animals are fun because the young ones know what they are searching for. Then get a bit more imaginative for older children, giving them a "pirate's map" with hints about where the booty is hidden.
- Travel Around the World—Label different rooms in your house as different countries around the world. Let each grandchild select a place to go and they then figure out how they could get there. They will have fun getting to their destination and doing whatever "activity" is set up in each room.
- Obstacle Course—Inside or out, set up an obstacle course in which players earn points for running down a marked line, performing tasks at designated stops along the way. (Examples might be doing a certain number of twirls with a hula hoop, jumping, chewing a piece of carrot, and similar tasks.) Pretend this is your family version of the Olympics. When you have several grandchildren, they love this opportunity for fun, competitive play.

Bring that fun into the present.

- Water Balloons—Remember the fun water balloon fights you had with your siblings? Kids love to fill and throw water balloons on a hot summer day. Don't forget to have a supply of water guns handy too. Videotape the battle and have fun afterwards, eating snacks as you relive the fight.
- Body Painting—Tell your grands you have an afternoon planned that requires them coming over in swimsuits. Let the kids have some time drawing on one another and on themselves with foaming bath paint. Then let them have the hose! They'll draw and squirt all afternoon. Have bottles of liquid bubbles and other sudsy fun available, too, like a water slide covered with dishwashing suds. No baths needed before bed this evening—they'll be squeaky clean!

When it's all said and done, we need to remember when we were children and bring that fun into the present with our grands.

STRENGTHEN RELATIONSHIPS THROUGH PLAY

9

I hope you see that I'm encouraging *you* to be a child again. Yes, you. Don't let age or health get in the way. You can at least be playful in your spirit. Model before your grandchildren the playfulness that will carry over into their adult lives.

> Live each day as if it were your last. Someday you'll be right.
> —Barbara Johnson, *Mama, Get the Hammer!*

My husband, Rob, encourages the playfulness in me. In fact, that's one of the things that first attracted me to him. One of our very first dates in college was going to the park where we ended up covering each other with glorious fall-colored leaves. I was so drawn to his playful, fun spirit. He made me laugh—really laugh—those throw-your-head-back big belly laughs.

Oh, and since I'd never seen a palm tree, Rob even brought a live one in a pot back to school for me after he returned from Miami, Florida, from Christmas break. No wonder I was so attracted to this fun guy. I then was the only girl on campus with a palm tree growing in her dorm room. I just never knew what he might do! I hope he never loses his playful ways, no matter how old we grow together. I think it's good for us to keep playfulness in our marriage for our grown children to see, as well as for the grandkids now to join in.

Don't be surprised if numerous relationship-strengthening benefits start showing up with you and your grandchild if you're playing more with them. Here's a summary of what I mean:

- Play is a wonderful stress reducer in any family.
- Play is a boredom buster.
- Play sends a message: *I want to spend time with you!*
- Play affords opportunities to be your grandchild's cheerleader.
- Play can teach important social, intellectual, and physical skills.
- Play says, *I love you and value you.*
- Play lets you giggle, rejoice, and have a good time, making good visual and audio memories that your grands will carry with them for a lifetime. F-U-N—not a bad thing to be remembered for, is it?

THINK BACK TO THE GAMES YOU USED TO PLAY

"When I was your age . . ." Sentences beginning with that phrase usually have a negative connotation. When grandkids hear lines like that, they often think they are going to have to listen to yet another story of how Grandpa had to walk five miles to school each day . . . through five feet of snow . . . uphill . . . both ways . . . or some other hardships endured.

They will be fascinated to hear your stories and picture you as a child their age.

Yet, when you preface a sentence with that phrase and end it with: My *favorite game when I was a kid was* . . . , they usually sit up and listen. Children today actually are taken in by games that do not include sitting at the computer. Oh, don't get me wrong, I think we need to be very computer savvy and know the most we can to keep up in our computer world. But, think back on when you were a kid or when your children were young.

I still remember the day my 95-year-old Grandma Gladys chuckled and said, "I used to play basketball, you know, back in the 1920s. In fact, I still do! I roll up my dirty laundry and shoot it into the bathtub!"
—Laurie Windslow Sergeants, an Iowa grandmother

Sports were not so competitive and didn't start in early childhood like they do now. Play used to be much less organized than it is today. Why, if you were like me, you even only had one pair of sneakers. They were just good ol' all-purpose tennis shoes. Think back on some games that you can share with your grandchildren. They will be fascinated to hear your stories and picture you as a child their age playing games.

Here are some games and activities I am already initiating with my grandchildren that bring back such fond memories:

- Button, Button, Who's Got the Button?—Already a favorite with my grands, one player hides the button and the others look for it.
- Pick-Up Sticks—Players pick up slender, plastic sticks (you can buy these inexpensively at a toy store) of a chosen color one by one without touching any of the other sticks. When the player touches someone else's sticks, his turn ends. Whoever picks up all their sticks first is the winner.
- Capture the Flag—Each member of two teams has a hanky or scarf. The object is to capture all the scarves of the other team without getting tagged while doing so.
- "Hide-and-Seek"—One person is "It" and counts to 100 (or 10 if the kids are young) while the others all find hiding places. "It" goes in search of all the players who are hiding. (Adults make this fun when they walk right past giggling participants who think they're not being seen.)
- Hopscotch—Draw a hopscotch graph on the driveway or sidewalk. Each player in turn throws a rock to one of the numbered squares. Players must avoid that square as they hop to the end of the graph.
- Cat's Cradle—Two players interactively create intricate patterns with a long, continuous string or yarn that is stretched tight in the other player's hands.
- Kick the Can—This game requires nothing more than a can that is kicked as far as possible by one of the players. The person who is "It" has to bring the can back to its original place, while other players hide. Then "It" has to find the hiders; but if one of them darts out and kicks the can without being tagged, "It" has to start all over again.
- Dress-up—Preschoolers, especially, love to dress up in Cinderella gowns, ballerina tutus, or just anything you may have in a dress-up box. Playing in these clothes gives children a way to experiment with adult roles and practice social interactions that mimic the adult world. And it's so fun to join in! You wouldn't believe some of the outfits from my dress-up box that the grandchildren have dressed *me* in! Take the children's pictures and then sit together going over

the silliness and giggling together at "rest time." Shop yard sales for cool items. Wedding veils, hats, jewelry, and big, swirly dresses are absolutely the best. Have a plastic storage tub full for them when they come over.

- Tea Parties—Dress up and have an old-fashioned Victorian tea complete with china cups, fancy napkins, and dainty cookies. Little girls and, yes, even our grandson, just love these parties. Sometimes we sit under the trees in our backyard; other times, we get quite formal with a lace tablecloth on a small table in our living room. "I will pour." I love to hear them say that.
- Swinging in the Park—Give your grandkids a big push and hop in the swing right next to them! Leaning back, looking up at patches of blue sky peeking through the glistening green leaves and tree branches... watching the world go by. There's nothing like getting on a swing in the park (or in your backyard) to bring out the playfulness in you.
- What's the Object?—Do a taste test of a variety of tidbits to blindfolded players who have to guess what they are. Marshmallows, pickles, peanut butter, chocolate syrup, a dash of salt. You could have an endless list of items.
- Charades—What fun to bring back this timeless game!
- Lemonade Stand—Remember how the neighbors and Dad used to purchase cup after cup?
- Snowball Fights—Yes, even in July! Crumple up waste paper, used tissue or wrapping paper, and even junk mail. Have teams make a fort on two sides of a room and let 'em go at it.
- Roadway—Draw a sidewalk road in the driveway including familiar "landmarks" for the kids to "drive" their trikes and bikes to, such as stores, their house, church, or Grandma's.

I wish I had the energy that my grandchildren have—if only for self-defense.
—Gene Perret

Going back over this list of games takes me back to hot, humid summer evenings playing games in the middle of the street with a dozen or so neighborhood friends. I'd come home with a "dirt necklace" my mother would call it—beads of dirt and sweat caught in the wrinkles around my neck from having such a grand time outside right up until it was dark enough for the fireflies to appear. What childhood treasures of those days I hold in my heart. So carefree. When else in my life have I had time to make lightning bug rings and dandelion necklaces? Ah, such glorious adventures we kids had on that cul-de-sac!

It's the little things that bring children the greatest joys. I pray that I remember that truth and pass it on to my grandchildren. Oh, sure, sporting equipment and toys are nice to have around our house (and we do), but I'm discovering that it's our presence and undivided attention that our grands really want most from us.

> When we do the best that we can, we never know what miracle is wrought in our life, or in the life of another.
> —Helen Keller

Do these memories of your childhood make you want to go right out and have some fun? I sure do. (I wish we'd had the washable sidewalk chalk that is available now. I wouldn't have gotten in trouble nearly as much for marking up the neighborhood sidewalks.) Don't get too hung up on organizing the games and setting rules. The important thing is to spend time playing with your grandchildren. The games we play with them will bond us together forever.

Don't get too hung up on organizing the games and setting rules.

When grandchildren are playing at your house, remember that most kids are quite dependent on regular schedules. If a toddler seems to be fussing more than usual, think about whether or not it could be related to his missing regular scheduled nap-times. Teens are famous for liking to stay up late and sleep late. If that's their long-standing schedule at home, honor it at your house, though you might have to bite your tongue and forgo giving your "early to bed early to rise" sermon or "the early bird catches the worm" speech.

Otherwise, your teen grandchild will not be eager to join in when you're ready to playfully interact. Those hormonal waters can be difficult to navigate. You might be surprised at how cooperative a teen can be when they sense your respect of their schedule, eating habits, and interests. The more we can adapt our activities to our grandchildren's personalities and ages, the more we will enjoy playing with them...and they with us.

Arrange for Five Minutes of "Away Play"

Often when we're with our grands, they (and we) need a break *from* one another or *with* each other. I call it "away play" because of the break it gives both grandmom and grandchild. Acting out or angry behavior is often brought on by physical exhaustion or by a child's need to have all your attention for a bit. Even teenagers—maybe especially teenagers—can experience this. By breaking from what you are doing with the entire group of siblings or cousins to single out one grandchild for five minutes of individual attention, you may just be doing him and yourself the biggest favor of the day.

One of the great things about play is the opportunity to learn to give and take with others, but when a child is cutting up, not cooperating, hitting, screaming, or all of the above...it's time to step aside with him or her for a bit. Acting out in group play often stems from a child being overwhelmed. It's our responsibility as the grandmom-in-charge to step in, step aside with the child, and disconnect from the group a bit. I've seen it work time and time again. While the others lazily lie around and watch an hour of TV, you can take the child aside who doesn't know how to scream *I need* "one-on-one time" but screams anyway!

Have a one-on-one conversation with the grandchild you're sensing needs it the most.

Even when you're immobilized by seat belts in the car, if you're good, without the others noticing, you can ward off a lot of horsing around at your movie later if you have a one-on-one conversation with the grandchild you're sensing needs it the most.

My friend Jan and I were chatting about these strategies one day when she mentioned how her twin grandchildren would start using every trick in the book—saying they were sick, smashing the other in the stomach, and so on—to get her attention after they'd been at her house for an afternoon. Jan began finding that she rid herself of uncooperative grandchildren if she would spend some one-on-one play with both of the grandchildren at some point in each visit to her home. One loved to snuggle in a rocking chair reading a book. The other twin enjoyed making a project or baking in the kitchen with her. Jan says, "I can tell the precise moment one twin needs that five-minute break from the other and just time with me alone. Some things I do just with one twin and those things become 'our thing.' It really makes the child feel special. Their whole demeanor during the time they are at our house goes so much smoother with their knowing that we're going to have a regularly scheduled one-on-one time together at some point in the visit."

In the next chapter, we'll look at more ways to engage one-on-one and with groups of grands.

Tell Jokes, Spin Tales, and Maintain Joy

10

"Knock, knock."
"Who's there?"
"Olive."
"Olive who?"
"Olive you!"

Last month my little four-year-old granddaughter Anna must have told me that joke at least ten times. I gave the same answer each time and big hugs and kisses followed each time.

Sigh. Now I'm back in my own home. I called Anna last night just to hear the joke all over again. Her giggle over the phone let me know how tickled she was to get to tell me her joke again—although it was a bit of a different version this time.

Get some jokes of your own. Be a fun, even funny, grandmom. For those of us who usually forget the punch line, it takes some preparation. Here are a few I've memorized that I'll share with you so you'll be ready too:

Question: What do you call a receptionist in a beauty salon?
Answer: A hair traffic controller.

Question: How do you make a hot dog stand?
Answer: Take away his chair!

Question: Why are frogs so happy?
Answer: Because they eat whatever bugs them.

Question: Why did the frog wear a mask to the bank?
Answer: Because he wanted to "rob-bit."

Yes, these jokes are corny. But, you're smiling. I just know you are. Your grandkids will think they are silly, goofy jokes too. I know they won't be able to keep from smiling either. Everyone has fond memories of grown-ups being silly. I know I do, and I bet you do as well. While growing up, I always thought the silly thing my daddy would say at bedtime was really cheesy. He'd always say, "Shadrach, Meshach, and To-Bed-We-Go!"—even when I had sleepovers at my house!

You know what? I found myself saying it to my girls at bedtime, and now I say the very same thing to my grandchildren. My daddy's lighthearted, fun silliness makes him a joy to be around. I'd give just about anything to be a little girl again just for one night to hear my daddy say one more time what I thought back then was a goofy bedtime ritual.

Tell a joke or tell something funny that happened to you. Laughter helps us along life's way. It's what often lights our way in dark circumstances. Laughter is contagious and does everyone in the room some good, especially the laughter of a child. As somebody once said, laughter may be the cheapest luxury we have. It's good for us! Laughter stirs up the blood, makes the chest expand, electrifies the nerves, and energizes the whole body. Humor diffuses awkward situations and relationships. Have you ever just met someone and, not knowing them very well, found being together difficult and strained?

Laughter helps us along life's way. It's what often lights our way in dark circumstances.

We can even feel that way with our grandchildren, particularly if they live long distance. But, you let just one crazy story get started and everybody starts chuckling and relaxing around one another.

We can never get enough laughter. Every little bit of joy helps. What does the Bible say about laughter? "He who is of a merry heart has a continual feast" (Proverbs 15:15). *The Living Bible* says it this way: "When a [person] is gloomy, everything seems to go wrong; when he is cheerful, everything seems to go right." From personal experience, I know that to be true.

When going through a painful time in my late 20s, depression kept me from finding much humor in anything at all. When it got so bad that I could not find comfort in my precious Rob's encouragement or even in praying, I finally went for help. After weeks of hospitalization, months of counseling, and the love of Jesus saturating my heart moment by moment, I finally began smiling again through my tears. I learned to cultivate a sense of humor because it is so connected to the way we look at all of life. (Wow! Just exactly what God says in His Word.)

I learned that we must look for the joy in our circumstances. Even when our circumstances do not change, joy helps us to look at them differently. So I began to do everything I could to cultivate a sense of humor. I looked for humor in videos, cartoons, books, magazines, and even in people. I made a point of spending time with fun-loving people, not those who were dragging me down. Clipping cartoons to put on my fridge or bulletin board has become a source of humor throughout my day. I share them with friends by enclosing them in funny cards when I'm done getting a splash of joy from them. Sometimes I begin to laugh wildly in a card shop in the humor section while selecting cards. I have to then remind myself how to act politely in public, but it sure is fun to share a funny card with whoever is standing nearby. Often I'll glue an article, card, or clip from a magazine or the funny paper into my journal to enjoy it time and time again.

Something else that is a great jump-start to awakening humor and fun in our lives is to learn to laugh at ourselves. If we can't laugh about what we do that's embarrassing, we will remain embarrassed! But if we can share embarrassing moments with others, people will be drawn closer to us because they will see that we admit our own imperfections. Laughing together over life's twists and turns is a great way to release stress and keep it at a minimum. Our own stories also make great things to tell later. Here is one from my life:

> I dashed in to the grocery a while back to get a few items before flying out the next morning. Not finding my shopping list when I got inside the store, I just began to go aisle to aisle selecting a few things. Feeling a tap on my shoulder in the checkout line, I turned to see what the elderly gentleman behind me wanted. "You have something on the back of you, ma'am," he said. I smiled and mumbled that I'd take care of it later, but he kept tapping and pointing to my derriere. Finally I reached behind me and there was my bright yellow sticky note! I had marched up and down every aisle in the store with it flapping in the breeze!

I burst out in laughter as I pulled the sticky note off of my bum. Four people in line, the cash register girl, and the elderly gentleman all got a big chuckle out of the moment with me.

That story is now one of the funniest "most embarrassing moment" adventures I tell—second only maybe to the one about when I sprayed my hair heavily with furniture polish instead of hair spray just minutes before I was to be on the platform to speak in a church. Yep, I really did that. And my hair was so plastered that it didn't move for about two weeks!

Oh yes, and there's the time when I was standing outside our church shaking hands with members of the congregation as they left and a bird decided to leave a special present from above on my right cheek. You should hear our granddaughters squeal when I tell that story. "Oooo, bird poop, Nana!" What are you gonna do? It was bad. Real bad. We just have to make fun times out of the disasters that could otherwise mess up our whole day. To paraphrase the familiar saying, "What goes around, comes around—sometimes tenfold."

"A smile is the shortest distance between two people."
—Victor Borge, in *Mama, Get the Hammer!*, by Barbara Johnson

The next time your grands say, "Tell us a story," just watch their faces light up when you tell a zany one about you. Tickle their funny bone. As somebody said, "Laughter is like premium gasoline—it helps take the knock out of living!"

We just have to make fun times out of the disasters that could otherwise mess up our whole day.

One dear grandma friend shared with me recently, "Our grandchildren spent last weekend at our house, the first time we'd had them alone in two years because of a strained relationship with their mom, our son's ex. We knew that future visits were riding on this weekend, so my husband and I determined before the children arrived that we would make their visit as positive and fun-filled, with as much laughter, as we could. The entire weekend was so refreshing. I'd forgotten what it felt like to have a deep, gut-filled laugh! The visit was so healing, and I believe it was directly because of the fun and laughter. We'd been so beaten down and now we're beginning to look up. God is so good!"

Doctors are agreeing more and more that everyone would be healthier if they laughed more. God doesn't intend for us to live in a tense, uptight world. Proverbs 17:22 says, "A merry heart does good like a medicine, but a broken spirit dries the bones." We as grandmoms have the opportunity to give a powerful tonic to our families. A tonic that can heal. Many a godly grandmother has been used by God to help relieve the pain in her grandchild's heart—pain so deep that the tough blows of life have dealt. Like no one else can in a child's life, grandmothers serve as a reminder that "Jesus still loves you, this I know, for the Bible tells me so."

FIVE-MINUTE PLAY TIME-OUTS

As you can tell by now, one of my deep-down-in-my heart desires as a grandmom is to create fond and wonderful memories for my grandchildren. However, creating delightful memories doesn't mean that I entertain a grandchild 24/7. Kids best enjoy their playtime if you alternate their activities, not only playing with them but letting them play alone. I find that we grandmoms need them to play independently to give us a break too.

Encourage periods of "solo" play after rowdy group play. After creative play, suggest some downtime, just-for-fun play. When they've played indoors, bundle them up for outdoor fun. Interestingly, when asked to tell what their favorite playtimes were, the majority of kids of all ages listed the most simple, cost-free activities. Great-grandma Phyllis suggests making an "I'm bored" envelope containing various activities written on slips of paper. Her grandkids love it. When she hears "I'm boooooo-rrrrred," she let's the kids pull out a slip of paper for five minutes of a change of pace. I love that idea and will certainly have reason to implement an envelope of my own by next summer, I'm sure.

Five-minute fun stuff to do when "there's nothing to do":

- Dress up the dog in doll clothes.
- Jump on a trampoline.
- Draw a themed mural on butcher paper.
- Make jewelry projects using beads and string.
- Wash dishes. Provide a sturdy stool, plastic kitchenware, dishcloth, apron, dishpan, and lots of soapy water.
- Make craft projects with macaroni noodles, yarn, and/or glue.
- Make straw houses using plastic drinking straws cut into two-inch pieces and connected with chenille wires.

- Create stories with sticker collection books or pictures cut from magazines.
- Work on puzzles.
- Play in sand. Hide surprises in the sand for little ones to dig up.

Keep these supplies nearby for other five-minute changes of pace:

- Safe, proper sports equipment—Shooting hoops can burn off some energy for the kids and give Grandmom a moment's peace for a cup of tea. (Keep an eye on them at the window.)
- Bulletin boards, Bible verses, art supplies, borders, pushpins, and markers—Let grandchildren decorate a bulletin board in the room they stay in at your house.
- Matching items—Let the kids find the other half of a deck of cards, sorting shapes, numbers, or random pictures from storybooks.
- Potato and toothpicks—Let kids use toothpicks to hold construction paper eyes, mouth, nose, and other facial features onto the potato.
- Socks, paper sacks, markers—Let kids draw funny faces and characters onto socks and paper sacks, and then make up a puppet skit.
- Fingernail polish—Let older girls sample Grandma's favorite colors. Either let them go at it on their own, or sit down and pamper them at Grandma's Spa while the smaller children nap.
- Old photos and scrapbooks—Let children look at pictures and newspaper clippings of themselves and other family members. Update albums and scrapbooks often.
- Backyard "science" supplies—Encourage kids to use a magnifying glass to look at interesting bugs (even plastic ones), butterflies, or anything collected that looks cool magnified.
- Books, books, books—Have a stack of books available from the library when the kids come for a visit. Consider buying some of the favorite books that pass on your faith and instill values you long to place in your grandchildren's hearts.
- Internet and email—Let a child work at the computer if he's visiting your house for an extended visit. Be sure you have an Internet blocker to provide site protection. Sit within sight, so you can glance over from time to time. It's a great way for the child to stay in touch with parents while away from home. Consider investing in a Web camera, and become a high-tech grandma!

- Disposable cameras and/or digital camera—Make one or both available for five minutes or so—especially if you and your grandchild are separated by many miles. Let older children use your camera or video camera to capture sights at your house and make a video scrapbook tape later of their filming.
- Baking supplies—Let children work together to bake goodies. Older children love to do the measuring and mixing, and then you can step in when it's time to use the stove or oven. Keep recipes simple. Older granddaughters will enjoy making their own recipe box and filling it with Grandma's recipes.
- Holiday decorations and craft supplies—Encourage five-minute breaks during Christmastime to decorate the low areas on your (or their) tree; watch a holiday movie; do Christmas crafts (use an online search engine to find crafts), and create Christmas cards.

Books are like sparklers. They light up your life.
—Janet Teitsort, an Indiana grandmom

HELP ME TO PLAY, LORD
Lord, I know that a child's work is to play.
So help me to be quick to stop what I'm doing to play with the grandkids whenever they say, "Play with me, Nana."
Lord, help me not to hear those words as interruptions.
Rather, help me to hear them as a special invitation into their world.
Help me to feel honored that they want to take me there.
Lord, while we are playing, help me to realize that at no other time will my grandchildren be this receptive to me.
Help me to seize these chances to teach them things, important things like taking turns and sharing and caring for other's feelings.
Lord, help me to be silly when I'm inclined to be sensible.
Help me to cultivate in my home a rich life, full of fun, music, play, imagination, and lots of laughter.
Lord, help me to use opportunities of play to affirm my grandkids' importance to me, to our family, and most of all, to You. Amen.
—Angie Peters, *Celebrate Home*

I'm grateful to my friend Angie for letting me adapt her prayer for moms into a prayer for grandmothers. It's been a blessing to me—a great reminder to plan for and make play happen, especially on days when I think I might be too busy with my grown-up life. I've typed out the prayer and laminated it as a bookmark for my Bible. You might want to do the same, placing in line three the name your grands call you like I did. You'll be a better grandma if you do, because every prayer matters to God . . . even prayers about play. Only God can change the heart of a grandchild; only God can change the heart of a grandmother.

I do hope this chapter helps you put some zest and more fun into your life.

Go ahead. Collect some joy and spread it around.

Smile a little (a lot) more.

Learn a couple of new jokes.

Get out the craft sticks, scissors, glue, and glitter.

Come on, you can do it! You can at least try *a few* of the fun ideas in this chapter.

You will make marvelous memories with your grands by investing time in their lives . . . memories that will outlast you.

Every prayer matters to God . . . even prayers about play.

And have fun! My guess is that you will come up with your own fun projects for the special children who add so much joy to your life. Remember, the legacy you leave is the one you're living. Make it full of fun! I am grateful to Sherrie Eldridge for the following fun story.

There they were, four of our grandchildren seated around our kitchen table waiting to be fed. Four-year-old Cole slid onto the chair beside his big brothers, Austin and Blake. Ellie, dressed in her pink ball gown and hat, with painted pink cheeks and lips, looked like a lady-in-waiting.

This scene had occurred often during their visits to us, but today something was different. It was as if I had an invisible camera in my hand and snapped a photo just at that moment. There was something about that moment that made me want to capture it in my heart forever.

Was it their cherub faces? Was it their self-forgetfulness? Their complete dependence and trust?

I thought of Mary, who after her Son was born *"treasured up all these things and pondered them in her heart"* (Luke 2:19 NIV).

That is my privilege also as a grandmother!

It is so easy to get caught up in the daily humdrum of life and miss these precious moments that will never return in the same way again.

Seeing their faces reminded me of what is really important in life.
—Sherrie Eldridge, an Indiana grandmother

If you're looking for more ways to connect with your grandchildren, hang in there for the next chapter. It's loaded with a wealth of wisdom just for you from remarkable grandmas with years of experience. I'm grateful to these women from all over the world who have generously shared their stories and insights with me. They've asked me to share them with you. What they have to say will keep your battery charged even on days when optimism and energy run low.

Those experiences (fun with grandparents) are like money in the bank—it's there to draw on whenever I need it. And over the years, I have needed it.
—James Parkel, 2002 president, AARP, quoted by Willard Scott

TAKE 29 TIPS FROM VETERAN GRANDMOMS

11

In this chapter, I pose questions commonly asked by grandmothers I surveyed for this book or questions that have been raised in my own mind since becoming a grandmother. I've matched these questions up with tips gathered from grandmothers from all over the world who volunteered their answers and best ideas for this book. They are divided.... I know you will be inspired as I have been by their vast amount of wit, wisdom, and time-tested ways to enjoy this marvelous blessing of grandmothering.

These pages will serve to furnish as a foundation for all of us as we live out our faith in Christ before our grandchildren whether we've been grandmothering many years or just starting out. We will hopscotch through a myriad of issues beginning with the first question, which reminds us all to have a spiritual heritage of faith and love. These grandmoms whose words you'll read do not pretend to be perfect or know it all, by any means. As you read their words and look into their hearts, hopefully you'll get a glimpse of the Savior.

FAITH ISSUES

Q: *I want to teach my grandchildren, even in their early ages, that my faith in God has a very important place in my life. What do you find have been some practical day-to-day, workable ways to blend biblical principles and precepts into a child's everyday living?*

A: I have eight grandchildren. Before moving to Tennessee, I lived in Florida, close to six of my grandchildren. I began caring for my three grandsons when they each turned two months. I am grateful that both parents were supportive of my efforts to teach their boys the way of God. While I cared for the two oldest boys, they went to a church preschool where they received good training as well. I would pick them up from school, and every day, we would have Bible reading and prayer as soon as we got home. We learned verses, the books of the Bible, songs, and Bible stories straight from the Bible. We started in Genesis and went through the entire Old Testament. Nicholas, the baby, was too young to participate, but he was always present as we studied. One day, when he was about two years old, the pastor came to visit us. Nicholas immediately went into the playroom and chose a book for the pastor to read to him. It was *The Preschooler's Bible*! Of all the books on the shelf, he knew which one was appropriate.

We grandmothers must be consistent and always aware that the youngsters are observing us carefully. Now we have a chance to correct the mistakes we made as mothers! Always do what is best for the child and not just what the child wants. I have always been lovingly firm with my grandsons, and they knew that they needed to obey and behave respectfully when in my care. I often reminded them that the Lord was watching and expected them to please Him in all they did or said. I encourage them to pray for courage to behave like a Christian and also to pray for their unbelieving friends. It is a tremendous thrill to hear young children pray for themselves and others. Remember that children are capable of learning a lot, and we need to be exacting teachers. It takes much self-discipline, and although it is easier to simply play with them, we know what they need for their future life. We must not lose any of the precious time we have with them. It is a God-given privilege to be influential in their lives.
—Alice Hunt, Tennessee

Q: *Passing on a spiritual heritage to my family is everything to me. What is the best way I can do that?*

A: Prayer! Prayer reaps great rewards—it is my lifeline. My grandson, Josiah Stephen Perez, was born May 7, 2006, nonresponsive, and was brought back to life. He was in NICU in Palm Springs for about a week, then my daughter, Rebekah, and her husband, Ozzie, got to take their dear one home. I traveled 500-plus miles to help them for a couple of weeks, then brokenheartedly had to drive home to northern California. All the way home I prayed that God would allow our loved ones to move closer to our home in the Sierra Valley. Two and half months later, they moved—right into our home (along with the two college kids who were also living with them!). My husband, Craig, and I and our 15-year-old daughter,

Bethany, got to bond with Josiah as he learned to sit up, crawl, and walk—during the nine months that the kids were in our home. Now they're in their own home on a small ranch in our mountain valley, and Rebekah is on staff with me, teaching at our little high school. Josiah tags along to basketball practices (Ozzie coaches our younger daughter) and games, and he even went with me on a 5K run last weekend, a fund-raiser for our school's track team. By the way, I won first in my age division, and he (in his stroller) won first in his division, the baby division. What a joy it is sharing in his life, and our daughter is now expecting our second grandchild in just a few more months.
—Janet Holm McHenry, California

Q: *Often the biggest lessons our grandchildren will learn from us are the ones they learn from observing how we live our life. How important is it to you to live out values of your faith before your grandchildren, and can you give an example of how we can do that in our own busy lives?*

A: I remember my grandmother's long nails clicking on the table as she kneaded bread. I remember laughing with her until my sides ached. I remember how she so patiently taught me how to crochet, sew, and quilt. Grandma taught me about respect. I don't remember one lesson on the topic, but it was something that was taught through her life. I grieve as I think of all my generation is missing out on by not being able to spend extended time with their grandparents, whether because of broken families, distance, or whatever. What a privilege and honor it was for me to spend the first 19 years of my life with Grandma.

Grandma Splitter is my only living grandparent now. Since Grandpa passed away in March, I feel like our hearts have become even more closely knit. Grandma is my most faithful letter writer, no matter where I am. There's a long spiritual heritage on this side of my family. I can't think of one single person who has influenced my life more than my Grandma Splitter, both directly through interacting with me and indirectly by her involvement in the lives of my parents, aunts, uncles, and cousins.

I remember spending nights with Grandma and Grandpa. During their evening devotionals, they would pray through the entire family. That's not so much, until you know that they have—are you ready for this—7 children, 25 grandchildren, and 50 great-grandchildren. Well, you count that up. Seventy-five plus 7! That's a long prayer list.

I know firsthand that my grandma continues to do this, and this is coveted by me because I am in full-time ministry and know that much of the fruit is a result of her praying. I can't imagine what my life will be like without grandparents. But

I am praying that if the Lord chooses to bless me with a family some day, I will be able to instill in them the values and the faith that have been instilled in me through my grandparents.

—Kathy Frey, Missouri

An additional piece of wisdom on this subject from a *Back to the Bible* radio interview with Elisabeth Elliot:

> I just happen to be the kind of person who wants to dish out advice to everybody. Mighty few folks want unsolicited advice. So be very careful, and again, prayerful, as you give your grandchildren advice. If they're staying in your home, you have a wonderful opportunity to demonstrate to them what a Christian home looks like and how people behave in a Christian home.

MEMORY MAKING

Q: *As a brand-new grandmother, I am captivated with the joy of this tiny, precious life that the Lord has entrusted to our family. I want to get started on albums of pictures and memories. Where do I begin?*

A: I've found that beginning with journaling is the best place to start. Before each of my six grandchildren was born, I journaled my thoughts, feelings, prayers, and wrote a letter to the unborn grandchild. Then, when they were born, I wrote each one a personal letter to put in their baby book. To give you an idea, here is what I wrote to our last grandbaby:

> Dear Elsa Penelope,
> You were so very tired from your long journey into this new and noisy world. We first saw you in the Special Care Nursery, only about ten minutes old. I am crying for joy and just glad about everything. You are here, and Mommy is going to be OK. I have a new granddaughter, and my daughter is a mommy. When your daddy introduced us, he said, "Meet Elizabeth Penelope." No one has ever named their child after me, except my mother who named one of her dogs Penny! It is such an honor to have such a special place in your life. Your nickname will be Elsa, but you will always be my little Penelope.
> Later that day, I was telling your cousin, Stephen, all about you and he said, "Grandma, is it true that they named her after you?" "Yes,"

I said, "isn't it exciting?" "But, why did they do that?" Stephen inquired with a puzzling sound to his voice. "Well, would you like your name to be Stephen Penelope?" I quizzed him. "No way" he replied. "Well, then I am glad we saved the name for Elizabeth." It really fits you. And just a few minutes ago, I saw your little eyes focus on me, and I thought there is a resemblance!
—Penny Carlevato, Tennessee

Q: *I have kept cards and letters from my own grandmother that she sent me all through my childhood. They are priceless to me and chronicle so much of her life. I want to do the same for my grandchildren—any suggestions?*

A: I went before the Lord and asked for Him to show me a way to pass on my faith to my granddaughters. Then the idea came: Write Cassandra and Alexandria a weekend letter. I believe being a grandparent is our opportunity for a second chance at things we missed with our own; such as in our case, we were Sunday-only Christians.

I decided to use my letters for spiritual training. I pray over every letter. I pray even during the week for God to give me the lesson He has and is preparing their little hearts to receive. Each letter is unique. I am an artist and I use the envelope to witness to the carrier. I illustrate the letters. Most letters are very simple for a two- and four-year-old to understand. During June, I used our Vacation Bible School's emphasis on faith. I so look forward to writing these little letters. It has helped to know I'm planting seeds for a future harvest.
—Peg Nichols, Missouri

Another answer to this question:
A: As Grandma, Grammy, Nana, or whatever our cherubs choose to call us, we will impact them in some way. Sometimes we find they remember us for who we are rather than what we do. Hopefully, we are someone who draws them closer to the Lord.

I have two things that I "do." It is simply who I am. I write letters and bake pies. While both are simple and take little talent or ability, I am amazed at how few still practice these two lost arts. My grandchildren call me Nana-Pie. If nothing else, when they come to visit, they know they will always be treated to homemade pie.

I also journal and record volumes with each new Beth Moore Bible study. My oldest granddaughter, "Thoroughly Modern Millie," loves my jewelry and has informed me of the pieces she wants after I have gone to "be with Jesus." However, she recently said—even more than my jewelry, she wants my journals and Bible

studies. That touched my heart and pricked my conscience. As Beth Moore has stated, her journals are to be tucked into the lining of her coffin, with absolutely *no one* viewing a single page, I realized I need to "write with caution." Consequently, I have purposed to be positive and encouraging in everything I write, with the awareness that it will be read by someone I want to influence for Christ. So, one day, my oldest granddaughter will be wearing my jewelry, baking my secret pie recipes (she plans to open a pie shop with my special recipes), and reading about my walk (or lack of it) with Christ. That's quite a responsibility.
—Sandie Powell, New Mexico

Another answer:
A: On one of my many sleepless, prayerful nights, the Lord spoke to my heart as I prayed for each of my five grandchildren. He impressed upon me the great responsibility of being a grandparent. I cried out to Him, *"Lord, what would You have me to do?"* He answered, *"In your quest to write for Me, you have missed the greatest opportunity—your grandchildren."*

One thought led to another. As the Lord and I communed that night, I awoke the next morning and created "Nana's Newsletter." I gathered coloring papers, jokes, riddles, and wrote a personal letter, explaining that this newsletter would arrive every month. I inserted Scripture for them to memorize and told them to write to me and tell me all about themselves. I included a self-addressed, stamped postcard. Since postcards are small and simple, the children would not have to bother their parents to help them with the mailing.
—Carolee Reich, Pennsylvania

Q: *My husband and I are on a fixed income budget, so I try to make a lot of the gifts I give my young grandchildren. Everything seems to mean a lot to my kids. Any new ideas I could try?*

A: Here are a few homemade suggestions that are just darling. Grandma Debbie has the instructions in detail at www.extendedlegacy.com.

- "Thumbody" books—Our children have been thrilled at receiving these books for their children. Each book has contained the thumbprint of a different grandparent as the basis for the main character and is looked upon as a treasured keepsake. One book contains Grandma Deborah's thumbprint, one contains Grandpa's, and the third contains Great-Grandpa's thumbprint!

- Note cards—We began mailing note cards to our granddaughter just a few months ago. She is now about 19 months old. Although she didn't understand the note, she was thrilled to receive her first piece of mail and carried the card around for days crumpled and wrinkled, then wanted to go to the mailbox to get her mail each day after that.
- Bedtime boards—A couple of months ago, I tried my hand at making bedtime boards for the two oldest grandbabies (currently 22 months and 12 months). We gave our grandson's board to him when his family visited us last month. My daughter started him out kissing just one of two of the photos on the board each night before putting him down. He now *must* kiss each photo every night before falling asleep and has the best time doing it. She reports that he loves it. It was also her idea to add the holes and ribbons for hanging during the day.
- Grandma hugs—Give your grandchild a "Grandma hug" by taking a piece of fabric about one yard in length and attaching hands made of felt to each end. Your grandchild can then enjoy a hug whenever she desires by wrapping the "hug" around herself.
- "Life's Little Lessons" book—Write down some of the lessons you have learned in life and how you learned them. When the book is full, pass it on to your grandchild. It will become a treasure someday.
- Scrapbooks—Compile a scrapbook of pictures of things you have done together with your grandchildren, especially after vacations or visits. Put the pages in a binder so additional pages may be added through the years.

—Debbie Haddix, Ohio

TOUGH ISSUES

DIVORCE

Q: *One grandmother I know experienced the heartache of having her beloved grandchildren ripped from her by divorce when the mother moved to another state, and now she does not even know her grandchildren's whereabouts. For grandmothers dealing with the pain of a devastating divorce, death, restraining order, or who do not get to see their grandchildren for various reasons, how do you deal with the anguish that those situations bring?*

A: Long story short, many grandparents in pain have grandkids—some grandkids we get to see and others we don't. My addict son (an only child) has two children (my first and only two grandchildren), the first son he had out of wedlock and they decided to give him up for adoption—I never met that grandson. I pray for him often. He would be a teenager today. The second grandson (also out of wedlock with another woman, whom he is no longer living with) is now five years old, and although we live in the same town, I seldom get to see him for a host of issues and reasons. It breaks my heart.

I know I'm not alone in sharing the pain of a gram's heart when I speak about estranged children and grandchildren—there are a lot of us out here living in this situation. The only way to cope is to step up your prayers. Take it all to the Lord—He's the only one who can fill the hurting places. Then consider how you can give of yourself when opportunities do arise; that's the key. God has the power to bring healing.
—Alice Bottke, Texas, www.boomerbabes.com

ADOPTION

Q: *My son and daughter-in-law are adopting a baby soon. Any advice on how my attitude and demeanor toward this grandchild can be the same as my blood-related grandchildren?*

A: Our oldest daughter and family adopted a newborn baby last year. At that time, my mind was flooded with awe and adoration of this child, a gift from God to our family. At that time, I wondered if there was the slightest comparison of my awe and adoration to that of Mary and Joseph as they gazed at Baby Jesus after His birth.

Yesterday our family gathered for Christmas. As I watched Megan, now one year old, rip open her gifts with the help of her mommy (and then immediately chew on the paper!), I witnessed her delight in the gifts we had given.

I couldn't help but think about her position in our family. She is one of us! When she entered our family a year ago, everything we have became hers. She didn't have to earn it—it was simply hers because of adoption.

The same is true about Christ's family. We are one of His! Those who have been adopted into His family by faith in His finished work on the Cross are given His life, both now and for eternity.

Our attempts to open His gift may be childlike, like Megan's. We may only be able to rip and chew on the paper, but He knows the delight and excitement in our souls for the great gift He has given.

This baby couldn't be more loved and wanted any more by either the birth or adoptive families. She is cherished by all. Witnessing the outpouring of love for

Megan was an epiphany for me as I realized for the first time how much my parents loved and wanted me! This tiny adoptee's life made this a personal reality for this *old* adoptee.

After my daughter and I climbed into the backseat of the van and buckled the baby in after leaving the hospital, I began sobbing uncontrollably. Lisa tenderly put one hand on the baby and the other on mine as I wept tears of joy. It was a moment with my daughter and new granddaughter I shall never forget.

Because Megan was born during the Christmas season, my thoughts turned often to Joseph and Mary who were awaiting the arrival of Baby Jesus. I wondered if I was experiencing the eagerness that they were. I wondered as I wrapped gifts for Megan if I was feeling the awe the wise men experienced in bringing gifts to Baby Jesus. And as Mary and Joseph looked upon the face of their newborn Son, I wondered if they wept tears of joy as I did.
—Sherrie Eldridge, Indiana

WHAT HAPPENS WHEN GRANDMA IS GONE?

Q: *As your years of grandmothering pass, what dreams for your grandchildren do you find are the most important to you?*

A: Two areas I believe are vitally important. The first is to take the time to really listen to your grandchildren. Hear what is behind the words they say. Don't jump in with your opinions and answers. Become a safe place where they may pour out their hearts, hurts, and joys. Children desperately need to be really heard before they can be understood. Secondly, let your grandchildren know that you are praying for them daily. To my older grandchildren, with cell phones, I call or send text messages, letting them know I am specifically praying for something I have heard them say. To those with email addresses, they get regular messages saying Grandma loves them, is aware of what is going on in their lives, and is praying. All get telephone calls or hugs in person when possible, always with the message, Grandma hears, loves, cares, and constantly prays.
—Betty Southard, California

Q: *Could I hear from an adult grandchild about what in their grandmother's life has made the most impact on them?*

A: One of the most important lessons I learned from Grams was the amount of impact you can have in the lives of your children and grandchildren. My family and I didn't realize the extent of her influence until she passed away. Grams was

the nucleus of the family, and when she was gone, the dynamics of our extended family dramatically changed. This change was amazing to me, and it was then that I realized how much I wanted to be like her. I learned from her in subtle ways. She taught me the importance of my individuality, for example, by attending every single sporting or school event while I was growing up, even if it was 30° F outside and she had to sit in the stands. She taught me the importance of church by being involved in ministry and making sure her family attended regularly. She taught me the importance of faith when her cancer had relapsed and her body could not take another chemotherapy treatment. She taught me the importance of unconditional love through encouragement, prayer, hugs, kisses, "I love yous," and saying she believed in her grandchildren. I thank God for having such a godly, influential person in my life. She has left a legacy, and it will continue to live on through me, especially now that I have a child of my own.
—Melissa Beals, Iowa

Here's another:
A: Today, many years later, she still makes sacrifices and still chooses to honor God with her life. God used her life to influence mine—she placed my feet on the right path, and because of her leadership, my heart longed to seek after God. My husband and I are currently serving our first term as missionaries on the field of the Philippines! I would have never guessed this path for my life; there were so many times of doubt and confusion over God being able to use me at all, yet, He does! I feel that I owe my life to my grandmother—my Memaw—because of her guidance, her sacrificial love, and her obedience to God. She is my hero!
—Tina Ebert, Philippines

Yet one more:
A: My great-grandmother (which is what we had to call her—no cute nicknames for her!) once told me that when she washed dishes she always sang hymns, and it made the chore go by faster. To this day when I do dishes, I sing hymns and praise songs; it really does work!
—Joann Spain, Ohio

LONG-DISTANCE GRANDPARENTING
Q: *More and more grandparents find themselves living a great distance away from their grandchildren. We need some practical ideas to grandparent from a distance, so what would you suggest that has worked well for you?*

A: Grandma Debbie Haddix shares these ideas to make connections with your grandchildren:

- Color a page and mail it to your grandchild.
- Phone your grandchild. (Make sure you call at a time that works with his or her family.)
- Take photographs of seasonal events you participate in and mail them to your grandchild.
- Share what you are thankful for in words or pictures.
- Help your grandchildren learn Bible verses. They can repeat them to you on the phone.
- Record yourself singing favorite songs and send the recording to your grandchild.
- Mail a "Kiss." Send a bag of HersheyKisses® to your grandchild's parent. Include instructions that a "Kiss" be given to your grandchild every day with a message that the "Kiss" is from Grandma.
- Send self-addressed, stamped envelopes and blank paper to your grandchild. Include stamping ink, stickers, and pencils or pens. This makes it easy for them to write to you.
- Have a Valentine's Day "heart attack." Cut out several construction paper hearts. Write something on each heart shape that you admire/appreciate about your grandchild. Mail the hearts all together in an envelope to your grandchild to use as Valentine's Day decorations.

The following ideas require a little effort in preparing or executing. Directions and/or helps for these activities can be found at www.extendedlegacy.com.

- Add-on pictures. Draw an "add-on" picture with your grandchild. You begin the picture and mail it to your grandchild who will add the next portion. Continue sending the picture back and forth until it is complete. You might even make a copy of the completed picture so each of you can enjoy it.
- Personalized accessories. Decoupage photos of long-distance grands onto a keepsake box or other accessory item for your grandchildren. This is a great way to keep the faces of long-distance relatives before your grandchildren.
- Grandma's Bible cover. Create a personalized Bible cover using your grandchild's photograph and fabric. This is a great way for

Grandma to keep the faces of her grandchildren in front of her as a reminder of her biblical legacy to them. Grandma's Bible cover makes a wonderful gift from grandchild to grandma.

Another Great Idea from Grandma Debbie:

A new tradition is born in the Haddix family. When our first granddaughter was about to turn one year old, I began thinking of a gift for her that would be special. As I rolled ideas around in my mind, I remembered that she really enjoyed trying to sit in a doll's chair at her home. I thought that she might like a kid-sized chair of her own to sit in. Then I began to consider how I might make this chair something personal for our little girl. Eventually, the idea of incorporating photographs onto the chair emerged. Finally, I checked with Mom to ask what might be a good color for the chair.

I purchased a chair and sanded and painted it. I then decoupaged photographs of long-distance family members onto the slats of the chair. I also included photos of our granddaughter and her parents. The chair was a hit!

Last week our grandson celebrated his first birthday. Knowing how his mother loves family traditions and photographs, I decoupaged a chair in honor of his first birthday. His chair? John Deere green with John Deere sticker accents in addition to the photographs! Another hit.

Maybe it's time for you to consider beginning a long-distance tradition for your own family. What are your gifts and passions?

Q: *We have been serving the Lord in full-time ministry for more than 30 years. But now that we have grandchildren, we're missing family more than ever. What are some ways we can ward off homesickness and stay involved with our grandchildren while serving in ministry?*

A: We are missionaries, serving in Ethiopia, East Africa. Our two small granddaughters live in France with their missionary parents, Lance and Amy. The parents keep pictures of close family members on the wall in the hallway. They daily, or sometimes more often, pause in front of the pictures to review with their older child, Kirianna, that this is family. They also have other family pictures available to help her learn about family and close friends. I was recently looking for pictures on my computer while visiting in their home. Kirianna, who was watching me, said, "That's Great-Grandma," even though she has not been to visit her great-grandmother in many months and had not previously seen that particular picture.

Because we live on separate continents, Grandpa and I decided we needed to do something to keep a close contact with then two-year-old Kirianna (her sister is a baby). We began sending weekly email messages to her, including a picture of one of us relating to our lives in Ethiopia (Grandpa washing the truck or working on Grandma's stove, Grandma walking down the street with a horse-drawn carriage in the background, hanging out laundry, or other everyday activity). This prompts an answer from Kirianna, helped by her mommy, with an update on her latest developments. That, of course, delights these grandparents.
—Karen Auterson, Ethiopia

Q: *Technology is a great way to stay in touch. How can we use cyberspace to grandparent in the twenty-first century?*

A: Grandparenting is a great thing, and we so enjoy having five of our own! Two of the children are in England and will be visiting us here in Hungary in August—with Mom and Dad (our son, David). We are definitely looking forward to that! Three (our daughter's children) are in Springfield, and we do miss contact with them as well. But, thank goodness for technology! We use an instant messaging application and Webcams to play games with them and see them on camera. Last year when our only granddaughter turned three—it was like being there at the party as we watched her open gifts and blow out the candles! Our daughter is good about keeping pictures of us around and talks about us so they look forward to Grandpa and Grandma time when we are home.
—Patty Peters, New Guinea

Some additional ideas:

- Send email messages back and forth often.
- Set up a routine. Email your grandchild at the same time once a week.
- Create your secret codes and symbols to help you illustrate messages.
- Coordinate a time when you will both have access to instant messaging.

- Locate appropriate coloring pages on the Internet and send them to your grandchildren to color for you and return. Makes great fridge art!
- Use an Internet crossword puzzle program to make personalized crossword puzzles for your grandchildren. Use memories, favorite activities, and information about family members as clues.
- Play Internet games together.
- Mail a CD to your grandchild containing a video slide show you have created.
- If your computers have sound cards, send sounds back and forth. Nothing cheers grandparents like hearing the voice of their grandchild.
- If you have a fax modem, send pictures, coloring pages, and other items by fax.

Q: *Many families only see each other once a year or less because they are living literally all over the world. What advice would you give to these families?*

A: I'll soon have 19 grandkids on four continents—and we are not where any of them are. All are under 11 years of age. At first I took it as a challenge and said, "I will keep in touch with each one." I send each of them a birthday card with a $1 bill; a Valentine's Day card with a $1 bill; and for Easter, I send $2 bills—just to be different. I try to send a Christmas gift to each one. If I can't because of distance, I send a $5 or a $10 bill. I also make cards sometimes with our picture on the back so they know which Grandma and Grandpa these came from. I collect coins from the different countries I live in for each of them and they love them. We call them as often as we can. I have been to Peru three times for the births of grandchildren. We really have to budget for this, but it is worth it to skimp on other things—like not owning a home of our own. I also write weekly family emails and share everyone's news as they sometimes find it difficult to share with each other in their very busy lives. This helps keep cousins in touch also. I try to make every visit that I am with them special by giving them one-on-one time. That may sound simple, but it is a solution I can live with.

One of my relatives commented, "How can you leave your precious grandkids and go somewhere else in the world to live? They'll think you don't love them, and you will miss all the cute things they say and do."

My answer? "I will have all eternity with them as they are all in Christian homes, and if I don't go to unreached people, most of those boys and girls and mommies will never have an opportunity to got to heaven." By the way, my very

serious husband is adored by all the grandkids because he still does "Donald Duck" when he talks to them in person and on the phone. They don't understand him but they giggle themselves silly and try to copy him.
—Carrie Liles, United Kingdom

Q: *Because I'm a grandmother who lives farther away from all my grandchildren than a second set of grandparents does, what are some good ways to make sure those grandchildren know the love is still as strong as their other grandparents?*

A: My son was 28 before he married, so I knew I'd have to wait before knowing what it felt like to be a "Marmie." When my grandson Jacob was born three years later, I didn't quite know what to feel as I live many states away from them (me in Tennessee and they in Texas). When I held him for the first time in the Dallas airport, I was stunned at the love that flowed from my heart. I actually spoke to a total stranger standing nearby and said, "This is my grandson." Of course, he looked at me like I was nuts! What does he know, right? I'm a long-distance grandmother and it's the most heartbreaking and difficult role I have. I want to be there for my grandchildren, to hold them, play with them, read to them, but I can't. Jacob is now 2½, and baby Benjamin is seven months old. I call them often, but every Monday morning I write them a letter, add stickers and smiley faces, draw pictures for them to color, and sometimes include a dollar for each of them. Their mom and dad tell me that Jacob looks for *his* letter from his Marmie every week. Soon I will send tapes, but for now, Jacob is enjoying his letters, and I am feeling more and more connected to them. There is nothing like a grandmother's love—it crosses many miles and loses none of its power!
—Midge Doelling, Tennessee

Q: *Often my grandchildren want me all to themselves and wish they did not have to share me with siblings or cousins. What have you found helpful to do one-on-one with grandchildren?*

A: Ideas for just-the-two-of-you dates with a grandchild:

- Share a hobby together—whether collecting stamps or teacups.
- Volunteer together for public service—from feeding the homeless to visiting the sick.
- Enjoy a day at your workplace together—giving your grandchild a behind-the-scenes tour.

- Put together a recipe book of family favorites, including a photo of each contributor.
- Join a church choir, drama group, or Bible class together.
- Plant a flower or vegetable garden together.
- Plan a surprise party for a family member, including decorations, food, and favors.

—Karen O'Connor, California

Q: *Since my grandchildren all live a great distance away, I feel like I miss out on so much of the activities and firsthand grandmothering blessings. I would love to feel like I'm still pouring my life into a child's life one-on-one. How could I do that?*

A: My young grandchildren live in other states, none close to Tennessee. I am practicing how to be a better grandmother with my little 8-year-old friend and neighbor, Grace. When I visited my mom over Memorial Day, playing with Grace in the sprinkler was awkward for this almost-59-year-old grandmother, but once I got into the playing part, it was loads of fun. We used a huge ball I had bought her that day and tossed it back and forth—part of her rules. Then we had to run through the sprinkler. Seeing her little eyes sparkle and hearing her laughter was worth the initial uncomfortable feeling. Later we played dominoes, and after the first game, I allowed her to make up new rules. That game turned out to be the most fun I've had with dominoes in years.

A few days after we returned from Florida, Grace's dad drove by the house as I was putting on my lawn-mowing shoes. Grace waved from the backseat. While I put our huge dog, Lady, in the backyard, Grace walked down the street. When I looked up she was standing at the gate smiling only the way she can. Normally, my first reaction would have been *Maaaaaaaaan, I've got to get this work done.* Instead, I invited her in, handed Lady's leash to her, ran into the house, and got Grace a bottle of water and Lady's favorite rubber bone toy. She played with Lady as I spot mowed outside the gate. When that part of the job was complete, I moved Lady to the front yard, and asked Grace if she wanted to walk another one of my dogs, Nick. While I mowed the front area, Grace walked Nick all over the yard and up and down the street, staying in my sight the entire time. When my job was complete, we went inside to find our favorite flavor of Popsicle and to allow Grace to pick up yet another one of my dogs, her favorite, Annabelle. We sat on the deck talking about swimming pools, trampolines, dolls, stuffed animals, and her desire to have a dog. We ended up inside, looking at my special doll collection. She oohed and aahed over each one and was especially pleased that I allowed her to hold my cherished porcelain dolls, which are protected in a glass case.

It was after 7:00 by this time, so I changed clothes and she and I walked Lady to her house. It was a delightful evening, the most delightful I've had in some time. And for me to take that much time out of my afterwork busy schedule is amazing to me. I have decided that God has brought her into my life to not only learn how to be with little girls (all my practice is with boys) but to teach me how to be an active, playful grandmother. I think before school starts again this year, I'm going to ask Grace's mom to dress her up so I can take her some place special for lunch—just the two of us girls!
—Midge Doelling, Tennessee

Q: *My friend has a Camp Grandma in the summer for all of her school-age grandchildren. I have five grandchildren (aged 7 to 12,) and I would like to have my first Camp Nana this summer. What are some activities with the children that we could do? Any suggestions? I may begin with just a day camp.*

A: Good idea to start small. Don't take on more than you can handle. Possibly one to three days is the max when kids do begin spending the night. Enlist help. Plan ahead by freezing most meals in advance. A sample day: crafts, hikes, lunch—hot dog roast, storytime, swimming, outside games (i.e., tag), dinner, s'mores by the fire, and wind down before bed with a movie. Shop dollar stores for inexpensive supplies.

Camp just wouldn't be camp without these additional ideas:

- A camp theme, if you desire—patriotic, beach, camping, luau, western.
- Crafts—and lots of them—for most kids.
- Bubbles and water games.
- An art gallery including sponge paintings of the children's hands on a wall.
- Sleeping outside in your backyard.
- A children's book—read a chapter a night.
- Tea parties with dolls or stuffed animals.
- Camp T-shirts—the first day's craft is for each child to decorate one.
- Decorated and/or tie-dyed sneakers, caps, or visors.
- Bible stories and prayer together, talks about God as you hike outdoors.
- Christmas ornaments to save for that year's holiday.

- A parade—march through your neighborhood or campgrounds.
- Songs and plays—rehearse and act out a play for the parents upon arrival.
- Refreshments prepared by the grands for their parents when they come.

—Janet Teitsort, Indiana

(A camp for grandparents and grandchildren is run by LifeQuest Ministries—get information at www.elderquest.org.)

Q: *I'm usually not good with keeping peace among grandchildren when they fuss with their cousins when in my care. Any suggestions on how I can get them to share and take turns rather than be so competitive?*

A: One thing I do with my toddler grandkids (I have seven under three years old) is to play toddler computer games. They love it. When it is not their turn, they pull a chair or two up and watch. I have a couple of cute pictures with several of them climbing on my lap while waiting their turn.
—Carrie Liles, United Kingdom

Q: *When there is very little contact between my adult children and myself, let alone with the grandchildren, how can I let them know the love and dreams in my heart for them?*

A: I have nine grandchildren, two of whom do not live with their dad (my youngest son) or near enough for me to see them very often. This has gone on for several years, and though I know my son does what he can to stay in touch, I have made it a point to write to each of these two little ones (now 8 and 15) every week, just to remind them how special they are, and how much Jesus (and I) love them. It has helped to forge/preserve a bond between us, and they have both told me how much they look forward to those weekly love notes from Grandma.
—Kathy Macias, California

Q: *I am an old grandmother and will probably not see the harvest of prayer seeds I've sown over the years. Can you give me some hope?*

A: My prayer is that my grandchildren, future great-great-great-grandchildren, and generations to come will know that their grandmother thought of them and prayed diligently for them. I prayerfully hope that they will seek the God of Abraham,

Isaac, and Jacob and know Him as their personal Savior. I pray that their walk with Him would be the most important thing in their lives.

The urgency of doing so became clearer when I happened upon a letter from a young Christian lady who wondered if all her family was godless. Could any one of her people ever have loved the Lord? She then came across a journal written by her great-great-grandmother long gone and read that this faithful Christian woman prayed for her future grandchildren, even this questioning woman. Her heart was overwhelmed to know her very own great-great-grandmother had prayed for her salvation even before she was born. "I have no greater joy than to hear that my children walk in truth" (3 John 4).

—Carolyn Crawford, Tennessee

BLENDED FAMILY

Q: *As a stepmom who "inherited" grandchildren, I know it's not uncommon for step-grandmothers to feel left out. How can I find my place treading the rough waters of being a grandmom to stepgrandchildren?*

A: As a stepmother, in many ways you always remain an "outsider." Although I love my husband's kids and grandkids—I attend all their functions and stress over/pray over all the things I see happening in their lives—I'm really not in their "inner circle." Unless you're a stepmom that won't make much sense, but it's true so more often than not.

I get along great with my two stepsons, but if their dad ever died I'm pretty sure I wouldn't see them much at all. It's not that they dislike me, but I'm not their mother. I'm their dad's wife. Because of that I probably guard my heart a little since I know not to get too attached as I would if they were my own children and grandchildren.

Stepparents have all the burdens, tasks, and financial sacrifices of parents, but very few of the joys. It's one of those things that is hard for stepgrandmothers. My husband and I have been married 21 years, but it's still difficult where the kids are concerned. I've ministered to enough stepparents to know this is not uncommon. We just have to keep our eyes on Jesus and not on people.

—Written with love from a grandmom who wishes her name withheld

Additional Answer:
We call our new stepchildren "bonus kids." It has made them feel wanted and special in our family. All gifts were both of the same quantity and quality when

we got together last Christmas. I think that helped the newer grandchildren blend into our family and made them feel grand!
—Sue, Pennsylvania

DIFFICULT EMOTIONS

Q: *Becoming a grandmother brings up a multitude of emotions for most women when they realize their grown child is having a child. I'm really having trouble with the birth of my new grandchild because it has brought back memories of having a baby myself, a baby who died a few months after birth. Is it natural for memories (good, bad, or sad) to well up at that time if a child has died in the family?*

A: I remember well the torrent of emotions I went through on the day my first grandchild was born. It was an exciting, joyous occasion. But as much as I was rejoicing on the outside, part of me was crying on the inside. When you have suffered the loss of your own beloved child, every special event, every family gathering from that day forward is overcast with a cloud of sorrow that hovers over, often canceling out, the joy.

As tears of joy ran down my face, inside my heart ached. I kept thinking how excited Mallory would have been to see her big brother, Chris, become a daddy for the first time. She would have been an auntie; his number-one babysitter; and a great helper for his wife, Erika.

Mallory passed away at the age of nine—just five years prior to the birth of my first grandchild. The only thing I could do was pray that maybe God will let Mallory peak through the clouds to see new Baby Bailey and rejoice along with us from heaven.
—Teresa Griggs, Missouri

Q: *We don't get to have our granddaughter spend the night very often, so when she does, she's always very afraid. How can I help her overcome her fears at Grandma's house?*

A: When my granddaughter Taylor was two, she began having terrible nightmares and refused to go to bed at night, claiming there were monsters in her bedroom. So I mixed up a brew of lavender and chamomile oils, which help with relaxation. I told Taylor to shake the bottle well and spray it everywhere the monsters might be hiding. My daughter told me that Taylor sprayed it under her bed and in her closets, and within 15 minutes of lying down she was sound asleep. I made "monster sprays" for months after that. I hold sleepover parties with my granddaughters. They choose their favorite oils, and we spray them in their bedroom before bed. Then we cuddle and talk with the sound machine on until they fall asleep.

Q: *I've just called everyone I know with my big news of becoming a grandmother! How discouraging it has been, though, that recently I've been hearing from several of my friends about how they just aren't that "into" their grandchildren. They say their lives are full enough, busy enough, and they don't want to be bothered too much with grandchildren. What single piece of advice would you give to grandmothers who do want to be a good grandmom, but just "don't have a clue"?*

A: I felt like a few words from a woman who loves being a grandmom were in order here. I have a friend, Flo Damron, who always told me, "Just wait. There's nothing in the world like it! Being a grandmother is so wonderful!" Now that God has blessed me with two precious granddaughters, I know what she meant.

Our Mason will soon be four years old, and Ashley will be four just three months later. Both are healthy, beautiful, darling little angels that can warm this Nana's heart in an instant with a smile, kiss, or hug. Nothing is more precious to my ears than to hear them say, "I love you, Nana."

Shortly after each girl was born, I would rock them and sing songs about Jesus to them. Mason's favorite was "Do, Lord" and Ashley's was "The B-I-B-L-E." And now I want to teach them a couple of Bible verses my mother taught me at an early age: Ecclesiastes 12:1 and Colossians 3:2.

My prayer for both Mason and Ashley is that they will continue to love Jesus and accept Him as their personal Savior when they get older. Because I want them to live for and serve Him more than anything else, I'm praying a hedge of protection around them.

Little ones bring so much joy and are so funny sometimes—without trying to be. The other day Mason couldn't think of the word *sisters* so she came up with *girl brothers*. I knew exactly what she meant. A few days ago while I was eating with friends and family members, Ashley had her little hands folded and was asking the blessing on the food. Her little face was just as close to mine as she could get it without touching me. But her beautiful blue eyes were wide open as she was praying because she was making sure Nana's eyes were closed!

I just can't imagine my life without these two grandchildren!
—Barbara Keeton, South Carolina

HEARTPRINTS

Whatever our hands touch
We leave fingerprints.
On the walls, on furniture,
On doorknobs, dishes, books,
As we touch, we leave our identity.

Oh, God, wherever I go today
Help me to leave heartprints.
Heartprints of compassion,
Of understanding and love.
Heartprints of kindness
And genuine concern.

Lord, send me out today
To leave heartprints.
And if someone should say
"I felt your touch"
May that one sense Your love
Touching through me.
—author unknown

Never Give Up on Your Grandchildren— Or Their Parents

12

Every time we encourage someone, we give them a transfusion of courage.
—Charles Swindoll

Never say never

Every time I speak I meet someone who tells me she is at the end of her rope. She tells me my story resonates with her. My testimony includes experiences with an unforgiving attitude, bitterness, and pain that at one point made me feel as though I was going under water and would never be able to come up for air. People listen intently because they desperately want to believe that the hope I offer them is true. They want to get past their past, but they often feel stuck and helpless in knowing how to move forward. Women at all stages of life identify with me as I tell my story of abandonment and self-rejection, my struggle to learn how to be an effective wife and mother, and my downward spiral into clinical depression.

It is only by God's mercy and grace that I am able to offer hope to others today. With opportunities to crisscross this nation, I now share how Christ has redeemed all my losses and has seen me through a multitude of hurdles and challenges.

Revealing bits and pieces of my own life opens the way for others to realize their own pain and their need for God's healing touch. Oh, how I praise Him for that. Not a day goes by that I do not thank God for what He's brought me through. I thank Him for allowing me to hurt deeply so that I might have compassion for others who go through deep valleys. Precious to me are the broken and hurting people I meet along life's way.

I know God is allowing me in this season of my life to be as vulnerable as I can so that I might show others how they, too, can be recipients of God's amazing grace. I'm a walking, talking (my husband, Rob, would say amen to the talking part!) example of God's effect on a hurting heart. Grateful for opportunities to invite others to find light in the midst of their darkness, it is my desire live out Paul's words in Hebrews 10:25, where he tells us to *"encourage one another—and all the more as [we] see the Day approaching."*

With that purpose in mind, I traveled this past spring to communicate my story of forgiveness. At the end of my session, a woman nearly fell down before me. She grabbed me, weeping, tears streaming down her cheeks. She couldn't even tell me what she was trying to say for a few minutes. Finally, she began, "Thank you, Sharon, thank you. No one ever talks about things like this. Thank you."

> *I know God is allowing me in this season of my life to be as vulnerable as I can.*

Gaining more composure, she continued, "I would describe my fractured family as one full of tension, angry words, tempers flaring, accusations flying, everybody at each others' throats, all of us looking for someone else to blame. It's been this way for many, many years. I just don't know if there is any hope for me."

I listened, along with two ministry friends, to this precious, tear-filled grandmom as she shared her story with great difficulty. One by one, each of us in the small conference room instinctively put our arms around this dear, troubled woman of God. Sometimes there's just nothing else we *can* do. The story we were hearing was mind-boggling. How *could* one woman live with such pain for more than 20 years? Where, when, and how did her torment begin?

Her story was a cycle of devastating bitterness that was created in this family by years of prejudice, attacks, and offenses. It began when this mom, with the best of intentions for her son, expressed disapproval for his choice of a girlfriend. Then came the wedding announcement, and, desperate to stop her son from making what she saw as a terrible mistake, she threatened to boycott his wedding in hopes of preventing it from taking place. But take place it did and the births of two children followed.

"I was biased, prejudiced, and used very poor judgment in not accepting my new daughter-in-law. In one split second, words were spoken that still sting the ears of my son and his wife. I have paid the price for more than 20 years. Our whole family has. At first, my son tried to neutralize my offenses to his new bride. I watched him become exhausted, trying to make the best of a bad situation. He begged me to let bygones be bygones. But, every holiday, every birthday, every time we were together became a traumatic event because of my actions and attitudes. I wish I could go back and change everything. If I could, I'd be supportive and affirmative instead of criticizing or condemning. I would let things go."

Somebody ought to do something

Dear fellow grandmoms, may we let this precious woman's remorse caution us strongly. The censure and disapproval that this grandmom voiced down through the years has likely now filtered down to her grandchildren. "That's why," she went on to say, "I have not seen my grandchildren in more than ten years. My son's wife won't let them near me."

Over the years, this woman has lost her son, a daughter-in-law, and two grandchildren. A disaster struck this family, bringing pain to three generations.

"Sometimes my son stops by. But, he's always alone. I long for time with my grandchildren so much. Unless a miracle happens, unless somebody does something, I will never know the joy of spending time with them."

With this woman's situation being so explosive, you'll never know how glad I was to have a wise ministry friend standing just inches to my left who had actually been in a very similar situation in her family. I listened as my friend in her considerate, kind voice shared practical, biblical truths about how *she* had recently taken the first step in making amends with an estranged family member. God had honored her obedience. She is no longer deprived of family events at holidays and birthdays and is able to lavishly love on her grandchildren, her son, and yes, even her daughter-in-law—with a sincere love. Praise be to God! Yes, it's true, *somebody ought to do something*. Ladies, that somebody is you and me.

I've purposely withheld the names of the women with whom I spoke. My purpose in sharing other women's experiences is not to betray confidences. Rather, I feel certain deep down in my heart that there are women reading this book who have read all the way to this chapter and now may be saying to themselves, *Sharon, this is the one thing I have a need to hear. I've been encouraged by reading all the ideas, tips, and other women's uplifting stories, but this chapter . . . this one is for me.* At least, that's my prayer.

> Major progress in any area is the result of a series of small, positive steps.
> —Mamie McCullough, *Get It Together*

Not long ago, after sharing my story with an awesome church group deep in the heart of Mississippi, one grandmom came to me, looking for guidance on how to get out of the pit she said she'd been living in for many years. "Miss Sharon! Will you please hurry up and get that grandma book written! Some of us been livin' at the bottom so long now, we ain't sure we're ever gonna get to the top again. I gotta do something. I think maybe the only thing I can do is...I just gotta start all over again as a grandma, and I need to know how!"

She will never know how God used her as one more confirmation to me that we *all* need to be reminded of the truths in this chapter from time to time. Emotion washes over me as I once again remember her sincere words. This precious woman wasn't just referring to beginning again after the devastation of Hurricane Katrina. She was talking about her heart. Beginning again—and beginning with *her.*

That's where it starts—with the one who stares back at us in the mirror each morning. We all need a fresh, brand-new start from time to time; it's the only way we can look in the face of adversity and pain. Yes, we are products of the past— but, we do not have to become prisoners of our past.

Gazing down at the thousands of lights below as my plane took off later that evening, I became overwhelmed with that thought. Then it struck me. She's right! What better way to change the future than to change (correct) what took place in the past!

Somebody ought to do something—I agree.

That *somebody* is you! And me! May we not be guilty of waiting until *they,* the estranged family members, do something. No, if we want to be obedient to our Lord, we must examine our own hearts first and then do what we know we need to do.

Most often, we grandmoms will need to be the one to make the first move when addressing alienation among family members. Good judgment and timing are so vital. Approach your loved ones only after much prayer and Bible study so that you may go with the leading of the Holy Spirit. I like the theme Jack Wyrtzen, the founder of Word of Life Fellowship, used to repeat to his staff: "You'll never be filled with the Spirit unless you're filled with the Word of God." Don't wait for a "magic moment" to orchestrate a conversation with an estranged loved one. Listen to the Holy Spirit's nudging in your heart. Go with understanding and compassion.

Don't force your agenda; go with the intent of discovering the other person's needs, special talents, abilities, and dreams, reminding yourself that God loves this person despite his or her faults every bit as deeply as He loves you despite your faults. Ask God to show you His plan, His timing. Intentionally seek God's face in prayer about the matter. God tells us that we don't have to be afraid in Isaiah 41:13. He also promises in Exodus 4:12, *"I will be with your mouth and teach you what you shall say."* The goal is restoration and healing of everyone involved. Be careful not to push your opinion or raise up wrongs from the past or else the outcome might make things worse.

IT'S ABOUT CHANGE IN OUR WAY OF THINKING

In estranged relationships, bad feelings rarely are the result of a one-time argument or encounter or trivial event; they usually occur as the result of a lack of trust, respect, and appreciation between the two people. The heart of the matter is that those three fundamental issues are behind the small incidents that take place on the surface. However, most families concentrate only on the surface flare-ups, when, in fact, the way the two parties think about each other is the root problem.

Let me give you an example. I trust my mother completely. I know she is on my side. She will sacrifice greatly to boost me just a little. Now let's take a friend of mine. Let's call her Kay. She is great fun to be with, but she's proven time and again to be self-centered, willing to cause great harm to others just to boost herself a tiny bit. I enjoy her, but I do not trust her, and I do not believe she is committed to me or anyone else.

Let's say I've planned a tea party for two, my guest and me. My guest doesn't show up, and doesn't call. I'm left sitting alone at my tea table, having gone to all the effort to prepare, and the guest doesn't show. If it's my mother, I give her the benefit of the doubt. She is probably stuck in traffic. Or, probably some emergency has come up. For her to stand me up, something terrible has happened. Poor Mother, I must track her down and help her wherever she is.... You understand the run of my thoughts. If mother tells me later that she plain ol' forgot, we both laugh about it.

Now let's say it was Kay who didn't show. I am fuming. She has done it again! I assume she had something better that came up at the last minute. I assume that because that's her track record. She could come the next day with all kinds of excuses similar to ones she has used at other times down through the years. I would not believe any of them and would continue to be angry. Same situation, but my thoughts and my reaction are completely different based on my assessment of how much the other person is committed to me and cares about my welfare. Do you see the difference? My lack of trust, respect, and appreciation for Kay are the reasons behind my anger. The missed tea party is not the problem. The way two persons think about each other is the true problem that needs to be addressed. What must be done then, grandmom, is for us to change the way we think. Here are some concrete guidelines to help change thinking, which will in turn change actions:

- When in a disagreement with a family member, concentrate first on understanding the other person's point. Listen closely. After he or she makes a point, repeat back your understanding of what he or she was trying to communicate. Make sure you understand the other person's point thoroughly. Only after making absolutely sure that you understand the other person's point should you then attempt to explain your view.

- When you are angry or hurt by someone, stop for a moment and look at that person through God's eyes. He created that person uniquely; He loves that person deeply. Just as God wants your dreams and hopes to come to fruition, He wants to see that person find his or her path in life. Step back from the current conflict and consider how the other person looks in God's eyes. Your job is to be a light reflecting God's love to that person; your job is not to criticize, give advice, or try to control the other person. You can only control what you do, and your job is to be a shining light.

- Remember that your adult children and their spouses are grown-ups; don't make the mistake of trying to tell them what to do or offering unsolicited advice. You had your chance to raise your child; now step back and enjoy watching the young couple spread their wings and fly as adults. They'll make a few mistakes, sure, but they'll live. Especially with daughters-in-law and sons-in-law it is wise to ignore the urge to give advice or opinions. If you want to influence, do it by setting an example. Let your actions be a model on how to live.

- Remember, too, that God has sprinkled different types of intelligences among people on earth—researchers have found nearly a dozen different types of intelligences, and no one person is strong in all of them. One person may be smart in academics, another person talented in personal relationships, and another creative in the arts. Different intelligences mean that people think differently, react differently, and solve problems differently. Respect the other person's uniqueness and appreciate his or her talents; the other person may think very differently from you, but that doesn't mean that his or her way won't work as well.

- Give family members, especially in-laws, the benefit of the doubt. Don't take offense to actions and words that are not intended to be offensive. Laugh more; look for the humor in a situation. Be encouraging. Respond positively.
- When you are upset with one person, speak directly to that person about the conflict rather than talking to everyone else about it. If you need someone to talk to other than the offending party, go to God in prayer and seek out a professional counselor. If someone does do something that hurts your feelings or makes you angry, go to that person first (after you've calmed down). In Matthew 18:15 Jesus tells us, *"If your brother sins against you, go and tell him his fault between you and him alone. If he hears you, you have gained your brother."*
- When you're in the middle of a stressful situation, stop for a moment and say to yourself: *What does this person need right now? I'm going to focus on what my (son-in-law, daughter) needs.* Repeat back to the person what he or she has just said to you, asking, "Have I understood you correctly?" When you are truly concerned with another person's needs, he or she will sense that you really care greatly about them, not just about "winning" or about having your own way. Thinking of only yourself clouds how you will react in the heat of the moment.

LET'S GET PAST OUR PAST

Our past becomes much easier to bear when we see it through the rearview mirror, rather than projecting the past to be part of our future. I had always considered myself to be a good person, and on the outside, I was. But on the inside, I had allowed deaths, disagreements, abandonment, inferiority, isolation, anger, rejection, and losses to keep me from being emotionally or spiritually healthy for years. Only when I allowed godly counsel into the hurting places of my heart did I finally begin to heal. By allowing God to peel back the layers of my pain, I saw the true intents of my heart at that shadowed time in my life—pride, ulterior motives, and selfishness.

Anger turned inward always leads to depression. No woman living only for herself will be happy for very long.

For way too long, I had thought that life was all about *me*, with the mind-set that everyone should naturally take notice of *my* hurt, *my* loss, *my* pain...well, bless *my* heart. I certainly did not esteem others better than myself (Philippians 2:3).

Living for others would mean *giving in and giving out*. I didn't want to do that. No wonder I was miserable, depressed, and angry! In your own life, remember this: anger turned inward always leads to depression. No woman living only for herself will be happy for very long. For me, the wooing of God came in the middle of my deepest darkness of depression. I praise God for showering His loving care upon me, especially in the loneliness of a stark hospital room. I really don't know how I can ever thank my husband, Rob, and the godly counselors who helped me through the wasteland months with their never-ending honesty, love, and grace.

They all kept opening the door of healing for me. I began to heal emotionally and spiritually, discovering that I could grow from my past to go into the future: *"One thing I do, forgetting those things which are behind and reaching forward to those things which are ahead"* (Philippians 3:13).

Keeping score, having a selfish prideful heart, hoarding ulterior motives—those are not the attitudes I want to have—not ever again. I don't want to live that way, and more importantly, I don't want our family to function that way.

REBUILD FOR THE FUTURE

So what do you do if you find yourself where I found myself in those dark days? Choose rebuilding. Make a commitment to do a U-turn. Let God help you trace, face, and erase your past! It is futile to continually dredge up pain, reliving every harsh word, or to dwell on real or imagined rivals. Resentment will always hurt you more than it does the person you resent. While your offender has probably forgotten the offense and gone on with his or her life, you continue to bring up the past day in and day out, dimming your joy, clouding your judgment, and smudging today's potential with yesterday's garbage.

Forgiveness does not get the other person off the hook—it just frees you.

Your past is the past. Nothing is going to change that. No matter what has been done to you or against you, begin *today* to choose to get past your past. Rehearsing every hurt is doing no good for anyone, especially you.

With all the understanding and love I can express to you through the printed page, I want you to know that it *is* possible to move on. I lived in a self-imposed prison for years. Do not attempt to get past your past on your own. Seek counsel and stay close to those who can minister to your needy heart, those who are willing to tell you truth. God can handle your problem but you have to give it to Him. You have to let it go.

What situation from the past is robbing your present days from the joys of being with your grandchildren or their parents? Guilt, shame, self-criticism, grudges, or blame will never minimize the ache in your heart. Sweeping your "whatever" under the carpet will only be counterproductive. Any real and lasting solution will come only as you let go. Give it all, and I do mean *all*, to your heavenly Father who waits with open arms.

"God, I don't understand," is a good place to start. Girlfriend, we didn't know what we signed up for when we became grandmoms, did we? We did not know the potential for pain in our tender hearts, especially when it involves family. Sweet one, God does care and understand. He will not leave you on your own. Listen to that gentle voice: "I know how you feel; I've tasted bitter waters. I understand that deep pain in your sweet heart. You are not alone."

The situation you find yourself in today is not a surprise to God.

The situation you find yourself in today is not a surprise to God. For your own sake, learn from it, and then let it go. Every moment matters to God. He believes in you and hears every prayer you breathe. Start now; let Him write a beautiful story of restoration of your family. Nothing can separate you from the love of God in Christ Jesus—not even the pain in your soul. Hold on to what you know to be true about God's faithfulness. Christ is patiently waiting for you to let Him move you forward.

> If God is going to do His deepest work in you, it will begin with this (surrender). So give it all to God: your past regrets, your present problems, your future ambitions, your fears, dreams, weaknesses, habits, hurts, and hang-ups. Put Jesus Christ in the driver's seat of your life and take your hands off the steering wheel.
> —Rick Warren, *The Purpose-Driven Life*

IT'S GOD'S OPINION THAT MATTERS

There are going to be times when things just don't go as we planned. It's God's opinion that matters during those times. No one else's. Out of sheer obedience, relinquish control of your children, grandchildren, husband, and expectations that you're holding on to so tightly. I often pray with my hands wide open to signify that I'm opening my heart and all that is in it to the Lord. He may be asking you to do just that right now.

Whatever the causes, however humbling or even humiliating the series of events you are experiencing in your family, know that you can choose to either be bitter the rest of your life or you can choose to reach out to God, asking Him to make you better. He's waiting; run to Him, rest in the shadow of His wings. Don't for a minute think God has forgotten you. In the midst of that pain comes an unfailing promise:

> *The righteous cry out, and the* LORD *hears,*
> *And delivers them out of all their troubles.*
> *The* LORD *is near to those who have a broken heart,*
> *And saves such as have a contrite spirit.*
> *Many are the afflictions of the righteous,*
> *But the* LORD *delivers him out of them all.*
> —Psalm 34:17–18

God is not blind, He knows about you and your problems. He knows of those who are suffering from the loss of a loved one, the knowledge of terminal illness, the memories of childhood abuse, the strain of financial failure, and your particular pain. And His love for His children will never leave in times of trouble.
—Billy Graham, *Hope for the Troubled Heart*

Every day I make a practice of reading a psalm to give me strength for the day and as a reminder of God's powerful love. A psalm of David I recently read applies well here:

> O LORD, *You have searched me and known me.*
> *You know my sitting down and my rising up;*
> *You understand my thought afar off.*
> *You comprehend my path and my lying down,*
> *And are acquainted with all my ways.*
> *For there is not a word on my tongue,*
> *But behold, O* LORD, *You know it altogether.*
> *You have hedged me behind and before,*
> *And laid Your hand upon me.*
> —Psalm 139:1–5

David could not explain the extent of God's love any more than we can, for in verse 6 he says, "*Such knowledge is too wonderful for me.*" Amen, to that, David.

BITTERNESS IS A POISON

In her book *The Gift of Encouraging Words*, Florence Littauer tells a story of a young woman who married a man but vowed she would never forgive an injustice in the way he had treated her before their honeymoon. Her fiancé had written a letter asking her to find a car for them to use on their honeymoon. The young woman took offense at the letter and held on to what she felt was a rude injustice. Pulling out the tattered, worn envelope from her bag ten years later, she said, "I carry this with me always so I won't forget!"

Probably none of us has a letter like this in our handbag (at least I hope not), but I wonder how many of us carry lists in our hearts. How can God work in a heart hardened with bitterness and hatred? How can we ever know real joy if we are constantly writing mental lists of other's words, actions, and mistakes?

God warns us that bitterness will destroy a person's life (see Ephesians 4:31). We must learn to be transparent when we've truly been hurt and willing to forgive in order to keep our hearts cleansed from bitterness. Ask God to humble you to see any bitterness clearly. God honors humility. Isaiah 66:2 says, *"This is the one I esteem; he who is humble and contrite in spirit and trembles at my word."*

Forgiveness is one of the most beautiful words in the English language, whereas *bitterness* is one of the ugliest of words. Today, will you let God shine a light on any dark places of an unforgiving attitude in your heart? Jeremiah 17:9 points out, *"The heart is deceitful above all things and desperately wicked. Who can know it?"* Psalm 139:23–24 reminds us to pray, *"Search me, O God, and know my heart; try me, and know my anxieties; and see if there is any wicked way in me, and lead me in the way everlasting."* Sometimes the results of stubborn pride take years to show up, but eventually, you will discover that the greatest hindrance to our families is that lack of willingness to forgive them and surrender to God.

> *How can God work in a heart hardened with bitterness?*

Once during a radio interview I was asked what was one of the most important things God had done in my life in the past five years. Without hesitating, I responded, "A lot of pruning and molding, especially in areas of my life where my heart was in tension with the kingdom living because of unforgiveness." Let me explain my answer.

I can think back to a time when I needed to forgive and didn't even know it! I wasn't aware of my need to forgive someone who had hurt me deeply until I let God in on the problem and He revealed it to me. When He did, I was finally able to forgive my birth mother (for dying—even though she certainly didn't choose to), my daddy (because I thought he didn't understand my childhood pain at losing my mother), my new mother (for stepping in to be my mother; bless her heart, I'm now so glad she did!), and God (I didn't even know I was mad at God, but I was angry at Him for letting my birth mother die).

Can you see how complicated bitterness can get? My unforgiving spirit turned to bitterness that turned into hatred then into depression, which spilled over into every area of my life. It shadowed me into adulthood, threatening even my marriage to a man who hadn't even known me when my mother died. It affected every relationship I had with other people. For so long I had tried to handle everything on my own. Well, that obviously didn't work.

Jesus can handle anything.

Unfortunately, it wasn't until all other options had failed that I called out to God, admitting my frailty and crying out for help. God wanted me to commit my will to Him. He wanted my trust, even if I didn't understand what He was doing. I learned that we're not to put the emphasis on understanding; the emphasis is to be on the submitting to His will in obedience—leaving the rest to Him.

Now that my precious Father and I have a long history (almost 50 years together), I am much quicker to go to Him first thing. I know I'm not alone when struggles come. What a joy and peace that truth brings to my heart. Joy comes only when I don't depend on other people or this world for my happiness. There is great satisfaction in knowing Jesus can handle anything because He's proven Himself time and time again.

> For God hath not given us a spirit of fear; but of power, and of love, and of a sound mind.
> —2 Timothy 1:7 (KJV)

What you and I have to do is to submit our messes to God and trust Him with even the smallest details of our lives. That's not to say that all our problems will be worked out according to our preferences. But God does promise that He will work out everything for our good and for His glory. What could be better than that?

When our daughters were young, they would say, "Daddy can fix anything." Rob's heart would swell with pride when he heard that, knowing those words represented the girls' respect and trust in him. That's exactly how our heavenly Father wants us to see Him—as a loving daddy who really can fix anything. *Anything.*

No one ever said this life would be easy, not even grandmothering. My heart aches for the precious women who have told me the pain they are experiencing in their extended families. I try to remind them that God did say we would not be alone. He's promised to be with us every single step of the way. Yes, the very God who parted the Red Sea to give His children freedom, who gave Job back everything he'd ever lost by tenfold, who loved David deeply even though he was an admitted adulterer and murderer, who used Paul mightily though he had approved the killing of many of His people, and who extended to Mary Magdalene an unconditional love like none she'd ever known...this glorious God, the only true God, will do the same for you. Trust Him today, dear grandmother; give Him that pain deep in your aching heart.

> God whispers to us in our pleasures, but shouts to us in our pain; it is His megaphone to rouse a deaf world.
> —C. S. Lewis, *The Problem of Pain*

WHY DON'T GRANDMOTHERS FORGIVE?

I find that often women do not offer forgiveness because we don't realize it will help us personally as much as it will help our entire family at large. Perhaps we feel that if we offer forgiveness, we would be letting our offender off the hook. Not so. Philippians 2 teaches that we are to have the mind of Christ. When God forgives, there is a complete change in relationship. Instead of hostility there is love and acceptance. Instead of enmity, there is friendship. No more blame game or stomping our foot and insisting, "but he started it."

Is this really going to matter tomorrow, five years from now...or even five minutes from now? Good grief! Let it go!

It doesn't matter who started it. What matters is *who is big enough to finish it.* We have to ask ourselves, "Is this really going to matter tomorrow, five years from now...or even five minutes from now?" Good grief! Let it go! *We* must be the one to stand up and stop the generational cycle of pain in our families. Oh, as a side note, let's remember that saying the two words *I'm sorry* has never killed anyone.

Jesus is asking us to forgive people in the same way He does. In Matthew 11:28–30, He describes Himself as *"gentle and lowly in heart."* Matthew 7:5 admonishes us with these words: *"Hypocrite! First remove the plank from your own eye, then you will see clearly to remove the speck from your brother's eye."* Whew! Pretty harsh words. But they are words we need to hear.

I am living proof that forgetting our past is possible. There are things I used to brew and stew about for years, which I honestly can't remember now. Praise to my God! Things I used to think upon every single day of my life and cry myself to sleep at night over...they're gone! I could probably try to muster up a recollection of certain issues, but why would I want to?

First one day would go by, then two, then three days without ever thinking about my offender or offenses. No more making lists and writing them over and over in my journal daily—thank You, Father. Pretty soon...voilà! One whole week would go by, and I'd realize at the end of the week that I didn't even think of that person once. Then after a while, two, then three. Then, praise God, the thought was gone!

> *If it is possible, as much as it depends on you, live at peace with all men.*
> —Romans 12:18

> *Let nothing be done through selfish ambition or conceit, but in lowliness of mind let each esteem others better than himself.*
> —Philippians 2:3

> If you don't surrender to Christ, you surrender to chaos.
> —E. Stanley Jones, quoted by Rick Warren

I can just hear someone saying right about now, "But, Sharon, this is the way our family has always functioned. We play hard together and we fight hard together." Then I'd say it's time for a change in the way your family has always functioned. Come to terms with issues and enemies within your family before it's too late— before the grandchildren get caught in the crossfire. I fear that some children feel as though they are standing in a field with people standing at each end shooting at one another—bullets flying past them all the time. That is not right and it's certainly not fair for these young ones.

Notice the word *quickly* in this Scripture gem:

> *"Agree with your adversary quickly, while you are on the way with him."*
> —Matthew 5:25

We say, "But, Lord, you know what she did to me. You saw her, You heard those unkind words…"

He answers: "But I want you to be like me! Just let it go!"

"Whoever of you desires to be first shall be slave of all. For even the Son of man did not come to be served, but to serve and to give his life as a ransom for many."
—Mark 10:43–45

Let us obey God. Obedience to God opens up His storehouse of blessing (Deuteronomy 28:1–14). Obedience strengthens our heart as God shows Himself strong on our behalf (2 Chronicles 16:9). God has called you to obedience for such a time as this for your family (Esther 4:14). Radically obedient people are treasures to God (Malachi 3:16–17).

I challenge you today to get past your past. Begin rebuilding your strained family relationship this very hour. Be willing to take off the boxing gloves, putting on, instead, forgiveness and grace. Perhaps to your adult child, to their exes, to your grandchild's other set of grandparents… you know where you need to begin. God will show you if you are willing to be obedient to Him.

I challenge you today to get past your past.

Your loving gesture may knock their socks off, but that's OK. What better way to share the message of God's love than to be a changed woman like the woman at the well, who declared, "Come, see a man who told me everything I ever did." Or like the blind man who proclaimed, "One thing I do know, I was blind but now I see!" Other family members may be struggling too; by your taking baby steps to love them, you make it easier for them to join you on the path of reconciliation. *You* become light in this dark "whatever" situation.

Grandmom, think now of what sort of message your grandchildren get by observing the way you treat their parents. It is a solemn responsibility before God that we have as grandmothers to be an outpouring of His love. He will hold your hand as you walk in His way. He will help you bite your tongue when you are about to say the wrong thing (trust me, some days the inside of my mouth is raw!). He will help you patiently wait and have wisdom.

God is going to hold us responsible for demonstrating to our families what the love of Jesus is all about. Let's live it out! Watch God work. He will give back what you thought the years had taken away from you. Jesus's promise that *"with God all things are possible"* (Mark 10:27) is our inspiration.

We can forgive...we can forget. The secret of experiencing deliverance from the effect of the past is to keep our eyes fixed upon Jesus—His beauty, greatness, and love. His forgiveness is liberating! May we dwell on the abundance of His grace rather than rehearsing old failures, hurts, and painful remembrances.

DARE TO SURRENDER EVERYTHING

14

Sometimes life gives us more than we think we can bear; certainly more than we ask for. Things don't turn out as we expect...and we're not very happy about it. I've shared in the anguish of my daughter and son-in-love miscarrying three precious babies—grandchildren I'll never see smile, hear giggle, or be able to rock until I get to heaven. Grief came deeper than I thought I could bear—that of feeling sorrow in my own soul, but deeper still was grief from watching my own daughter and son-in-law bear such suffering. I did not know from experience what losing a baby was like until losing those grandbabies. God's ways are not always our ways. There are beneficial lessons to be learned in pain.

The unimaginable happened in the family of Oleta, a friend of mine. She did not sign up to be the grandmother of a special-needs child. At first, she couldn't get past her disappointment, thinking to herself that it just wasn't fair. Yet, because of her suffering and the way God led her out of it, she now reaches out to other people in a way she never could before. Her suffering has not been in vain. I've watched her walk beside people who are going through similar circumstances, bearing their heartaches, and encouraging them onward. She admits there have been days of denial, anger, and fear. But she also wants us to know that "God knows what He is doing and will let the painful losses of your heart bless someone else, if you'll let Him." Scripture invites us *"Cast all your anxiety on him"* (1 Peter 5:7 NIV). It is then and only then that our trials can make us better, not bitter. I've never experienced the particular pain that this grandmother has endured. That's why I wanted her to share her story. Because she is blessed to bless others, here is what she wrote:

Oleta's Story

Nothing thrilled us more than the day we received our very first "grandparent" Easter card from our son, Craig; his wife, Anara; and our four-week-old "grand-embryo." Our exhilaration was enormous! What fun to announce something so important and how exciting to know a new life was forming—our first grandchild. Our heavenly Father planned for and already knew everything about her already. It was great to know also that our son and daughter-in-law were in the process of moving to east Tennessee to be close to one set of grandparents. We were so excited about it all!

Because of our daughter-in-law's age, and since she is a neonatal ICU nurse who had seen troubled babies, an amniocentesis procedure was done at 18 weeks into her pregnancy to assure that all was OK. A nursery was being planned in their new home so, of course, it would be fun to know whether pink or blue paint should be purchased.

I will never forget my son's phone call or where I was when he called me. I was at our local craft store getting a kit to make an embroidered quilt for the baby, at his request.

"Mom, we have the results of the amnio," Craig began.

"And?"

"It's a girl. And, Mom, she has Down syndrome."

My world came crashing down in that moment. As I got in the car all I could do was sit there, completely numb. I'd just heard the unimaginable. My excitement turned to fear and heartache in that instant. I couldn't imagine what Craig and Anara were feeling.

"Craig, God knows all about her and she will be fearfully and wonderfully made in His image," I finally managed to say. I went on to mumble that I thought God chooses "special people" to parent special-needs children. Even though I knew Craig didn't want to hear those words at that particular time, I see now that he and Anara believe with all their hearts just how true that is. I see it too. God could not have chosen two more special people than them to be this special baby's mommy and daddy. They are amazing parents.

I wish I could say that was the end to our fears and trials, but five weeks after receiving those test results, our precious granddaughter was in distress. The placenta was not providing for her; she was in serious trouble at only 26 weeks gestation. She would surely die if not born very soon. "But, God, can she live outside the womb this early?" I prayed. By now, this baby had a name, Clara, after her great-grandmother, and everyone was praying for her.

Clara was born on August 8, 2005, three months premature, weighing only 1 pound, 9.2 ounces, and was 13½ inches long. Her Apgar score (a way of evaluating the condition of a newborn) was 9 (out of 10), which just shocked us. She truly was a fighter, praise God! She was so small that her daddy's wedding ring fit over her little hand and slid all the way up to her shoulder. But, she was fearfully and wonderfully made in God's image. Our first grandchild— what a gift!

God knows what He is doing and does have a very specific plan for each of us.

We could not hold Clara at all; her skin was much too delicate to even stroke. We were allowed to only let her grip our finger. It was scary to be in the presence of such a small infant. She really did well outside the womb, which was a miracle in itself. Because of having Down syndrome, she had sucking issues and a feeding tube was inserted through her nose so she could take Mommy's milk with the help of a pump.

Praise God, little Clara never had any major life-threatening issues other than needing to be reminded to breathe periodically, which I understand is normal for "micro-preemies." A hole in her heart would be surgically closed at seven months.

After 88 days of nurturing in the neonatal unit at Children's Hospital, Clara was allowed to go home, weighing 4 pounds, 7 ounces. A barrage of equipment, scary for her grandparents, came home with her. Anara was a pro of a nurse and so was Clara's ever-learning daddy. It is just amazing to me how God orchestrated every tiny aspect of Clara's life. He truly did know everything about her, exactly what she was going to need and where she would need it.

Clara's parents also now know that it was God's will for them to move to Tennessee just when they did, as the care and support for special-needs children far surpassed what their hospital in Florida had to offer. Jeremiah 29:11 became a very important verse in their lives as it is in mine:

"I know what I'm doing. I have it all planned out—plans to take care of you, not abandon you, plans to give you the future you hope for" (The Message).

How I thank God for that verse! When I was raising my children, I prayed for God's best for them, for His protection over them, and most importantly that they would grow up to honor and serve the Lord with their lives. I am praying those very same things for Clara and now her new baby brother. Little Alan will be an inspiration to his big sister and a great peer example as he grows and matures. Early in their marriage when Craig and Anara had first started to plan their family, they had discussed having one child of their own and then adopting a special-needs child. What they did not know was God's perfect plan to give them that special child and a brother who could be a little "tutor" to her.

I think if I've learned anything through all this, it is that God knows what He is doing and does have a very specific plan for each of us. He is an amazing God. I'm looking forward to watching our grandchildren's progress as they each grow in the admonition of the Lord. I consider my job as Mamaw a privilege to be teaching my grandchildren about God, telling them how much He loves them, that He has a plan specifically for them, and is providing for their future.

—Oleta Midgett, Tennessee

Instead of asking, *Why, Lord?* I know Oleta would challenge each of us to begin asking, *What, Lord? What do You want me to learn from this and how can I help others?* The lesson is simple. It's about trusting our grandchildren to God. Completely. Oleta doesn't sugarcoat her pain. It was real...still is, many days on this journey. She exudes an overall sense of hope as she reaches out to help others in the midst of their sorrow and similar adversity. Oh, dear one, no pain is ever wasted if we let God weave all the joys as well as the sorrows together into a beautiful masterpiece.

I BELIEVE IN MIRACLES

An outstanding runner in a major race shown on television lost because at one point he looked back to see the positions of his opponents. He broke stride, tripped, and fell. Let's stop looking back. Let's forget what has *been*. Let's look toward what is yet to be. Let's keep our eyes focused on Jesus until we get to the finish line! I promise you, it's not too late to change the direction you've been going.

I have read the parable of the prodigal son in Luke 15 many times, but it never ceases to touch tender places in my heart. A lump in my throat wells up even now as I hit the keys on my computer writing this chapter. Knowing that I am a recipient of that kind of love from both my earthly daddy and my heavenly Daddy colors how I handle every relationship and circumstance. Like the prodigal, I distanced myself from the protective umbrella of my father's authority as I rebelled against his direction. I, a prodigal daughter, foolishly sought out "a strange land" as a teen, going down a painful path.

My own mother and father both were merciful and had compassion (v. 20) when I finally came to my senses (v. 17). How I love them for that! How could I not reciprocate such lavish love? I cannot say enough about how much I love and honor my parents.

So, too, through obedience and acceptance of God's forgiveness, your heavenly Father is waiting to kiss away your past into forgetfulness. Completely. You have a choice—dare to do what He's calling you to do. One thing is for sure—a loving Christlikeness seen in you will affect your entire family. Bow to His authority; surrender your will to His will. The more we practice, the easier it gets! God has a specific purpose for every single thing in your life—let Him have His awesome will and way. *Nothing* is too hard for Him!

He counts the number of the stars; He calls them all by name.

Surrendering to the Lord is demonstrated best in obeying our Lord. After a night of catching no fish, Peter modeled surrender when he tried again at the request of Jesus. *"But because you say so, I will let down the nets"* (Luke 5:5 NIV). Did you catch Peter's wording of surrender? Because Jesus said so! It didn't make much sense to do it Jesus's way, but Peter obeyed. He didn't miss his miracle.

Start living in surrender—you don't want to miss your miracle. Obedience is what makes all the difference. Do you need to extend your open hands before God and let go of your "whatever" or "whomever"? Let's do it, sisters! When all is said and done, God's promise is that your obedience will reap blessing after blessing...decade after decade.

I believe in His love

An outstanding runner in a major race shown on television lost because at one point he looked back to see the positions of his opponents. He broke stride, tripped, and fell. Let's stop looking back. Let's forget what has *been*. Let's look toward what is yet to be. Let's keep our eyes focused on Jesus until we get to the finish line! I promise you, it's not too late to change the direction you've been going.

I have read the prodigal son parable in Luke 15 many times, but it never ceases to touch tender places in my heart. A lump in my throat wells up even now as I hit the keys on my computer writing this chapter. Knowing that I am a recipient of that kind of love from both my earthly Daddy and my heavenly Daddy colors how I handle every relationship and circumstance. Like the prodigal, I distanced myself from under the protective umbrella of my father's authority in rebellion. I, a prodigal daughter, foolishly sought out "a strange land" as a teen, going down a painful path.

My own mother and father both were merciful and had compassion (verse 20) when I finally came to my senses (verse 17). How I love them for that! How could I not reciprocate such lavish love? I cannot say enough about how much I love and honor my parents.

So, too, through obedience and acceptance of God's forgiveness, your heavenly Father is waiting to kiss away your past into forgetfulness. Completely. You have a choice—dare to do what He's calling you to do. One thing is for sure—a loving Christlikeness seen in you will affect your entire family. Bow to His authority, surrender your will to His will. The more we practice, the easier it gets! God has a specific purpose for every single thing in your life—let Him have His awesome will and way. *Nothing* is too hard for Him!

Surrendering to the Lord is demonstrated best in obeying our Lord. After a night of catching no fish, Peter modeled surrender when he tried again at the request of Jesus. *"But because you say so, I will let down the nets"* (Luke 5:5 NIV). Did you catch Peter's wording of surrender? Because Jesus said so! It didn't make much sense to do it Jesus's way, but Peter obeyed. He didn't miss his miracle.

God's passionate display of love on Calvary's cross is for all the beaten down grandmoms.

Start living in surrender—you don't want to miss your miracle. Obedience is what makes all the difference. Do you need to extend your opened hands before God and let go of your "whatever" or "whomever"? Let's do it, sisters! When all is said and done, God's promise is that your obedience will reap blessing after blessing . . . decade after decade.

May your tenure on this planet be characterized by your grace, forgiveness, and a thankful acceptance of God's purpose for you in this season of your life. Choices you are making today have such huge eternal implications. Never give in or give up on God. He longs to make you a great grandmom. How are great grandmothers made? Not in houses of ease and pleasure, but on our knees in surrender to our God.

Oh, sweet grandmom; never say never. The more I fall desperately in love with Him, the more I realize that God's love for your family is so enormous that He sent His Son down to earth to prove it. God's passionate display of love on Calvary's cross is for all the beaten down grandmoms, for all illnesses, for all births that go awry, failed marriages, senseless accidents, hateful words spoken, dysfunction, and for anyone's world that is falling apart. In Jesus Christ, you will find *all things are possible*. That is my deepest prayer for you, for your entire family . . . most especially for your precious grandchildren.

LEAVE A LEGACY OF SPIRITUAL HEIRLOOMS

15

In one of my grandson Jake's favorite bedtime books, *Goodnight Moon*, a full moon appears in almost every illustration. I've read it to him many times, and he practically has the story memorized. Dropping him off at his house one starlit evening, I diverted his attention from having to leave me (he never wants to—you know I love it) to the brightness of the moon overhead. I didn't realize that he had never seen a crescent moon before. "Look up—there's the moon!" I said. As he looked up, his smile left his face. With the most deeply concerned look I'd ever seen him have in all his three years, he mourned, "Uh-oh, moon is broken."

"It's OK, God will fix it," instinctively popped out of my mouth. He seemed quite satisfied with my answer, and into the house we walked. No more than 24 hours later, he was back at my house with me when two back wheels broke off of a truck he was pushing across our floor, I heard a loud, "Uh-oh!"

I waited for a meltdown. Instead very calmly Jake said, as if only to himself, "God will fix it."

I can't tell you the number of times since that day that I've heard Jake use the same phrase, *God will fix it.* Simple theology, huge message, isn't it? *"Lord,"* I now pray often, *"help little Jake to know that You are able to handle anything in his life. Help him to apply this truth to specific circumstances now and when he is older. And, Father, help me to remember that You are the fixer of anything in my life too."*

Often extraordinary truths about God are taught in the most ordinary ways. Because such moments come without warning and often at the most inopportune time we've got to be ready to impart scriptural truths, seizing those fleeting teachable moments. They are more powerful than we can ever imagine.

This chapter may very well direct the remaining course of your life...and touch everyone with whom you come into contact. I can make that statement because I've seen it happen in my own life.

Because I take my role of leaving a legacy of faith very seriously, not too long ago I made a commitment before the Lord, that with His help, the remainder of my life will be dedicated to ensuring that the heritage I pass along to my grandchildren is physically, emotionally, socially, and most of all, spiritually rich. From the mail that I receive and the 100-plus women I networked with in preparing this book, it is clear to me that a vast majority of women take their spiritual heritage very seriously, too, and have that same desire. Let's begin finding pearls of wisdom in everyday moments.

> Just about the time a woman thinks her work is done...she becomes a grandmother.
> —Edward H. Dreschnack

THEY'RE TAKING IT ALL IN

You, remarkable grandmother, can make the most of every moment when it comes to living out Deuteronomy 6:6–7: "*And these words which I command you today shall be in your heart. You shall teach them diligently to your children, and shall talk of them when you sit in your house, when you walk by the way, when you lie down, and when you rise up.*"

God wants us to be communicating scriptural truths along life's way...when we look up at a rainbow, when we stand at the edge of a river, when we come upon an overflowing parking lot and need a space, when we pause to ask God to help the hurting people in an ambulance when we hear a siren, when we pray for healing or stop to help someone who is hurt...*all along life's way being the hands and feet of Jesus before your grands.*

Believe me, they're watching and taking it all in. I don't know about you, but as for me, even though I'm having the most fun ever in my grandmothering, I've found my body losing the vitality of my younger years, reminding me daily of the simple truth that I am not going to live forever. I want to sow spiritual seeds in the fertile ground of my grandchildren's hearts while I can. Is that what you desire? What seeds are you sowing? What kind of spiritual influence are you having? How do you encourage your grands in the faith? Is your life a reflection of the Savior? At the end of your life, will you look back at a bountiful harvest from the dozens of seeds you've planted, having influenced your grandchildren to love your Lord as you do?

No matter how old or how poor we may be, we have an incredible opportunity to be an example for our grandchildren by showing that we have a clear, driving purpose that gives us a sense of worth and makes a difference in the lives of others . . . a lasting joy from showing love day after day, patiently waiting to see positive results.
—Phil Waldrep, *The Grandparent Factor*.

FOR RICHER OR FOR POORER
The old adage "Be it ever so humble, there's no place like home" is true. As your grandchildren see that your values are eternal values rather than temporal, they'll want to emulate your life and keep passing the heritage onto the next generation.

Money can't buy happiness. True, without it we couldn't secure the necessities of life, but there are so many things money cannot purchase. The greatest thing we can give our grandchildren, our love, cannot be bought. Your grandkids may wonder why you will be cooking at home while they visit and not going to the expensive restaurants where their parents take them. Or if they question why you won't buy those awesome sneakers for their birthday, sit down and have a chat with them. If grandchildren have grown up in an affluent household, they may not understand that your lifestyle may be different than theirs at home. They may somewhat resent your not giving in to their every request or wonder why you are not a giving person, if all they measure affection with is what you purchase for them. Let them see that your love is infinitely sufficient for them. All the wealth in the world would not show your love. If you plan to show love with materialism, kids can see through that. All the wealth in the world cannot purchase their love.

In simple terms, discuss the situation regarding money with your grandchildren as they mature, explaining that money doesn't affect your love for them. Don't let them try to compare the other set of grandparents with what you do for or with them. Try to make them see that giving gifts is not the only way to show love. Tell them about people who are too poor to even afford housing, food, and clothing. And that those people are appreciative and happy. Show them by example how much you appreciate what God has given you. And, explain that you have had to

> *As your grandchildren see that your values are eternal values rather than temporal, they'll want to emulate your life.*

wait for the good things that you have obtained in life. Tell your grandchildren about the heavenly home that awaits us if we place our faith and trust in God and how much you are looking forward to moving into your mansion. Let your grandchildren see what my daddy often quoted from an old hymn, "This world is not my home, I'm just a-passin' through."

> I am redeemed, but not with silver;
> I am bought, but not with gold,
> Bought with a price—the blood of Jesus,
> Precious price of love untold.
> —D. B. Towner, "I Am Redeemed"

Our society has created such demands and desires in children. Be patient with them; wanting more and more is not all their fault. Face it; we've been there too. Delaying gratification for ourselves has not always been easy, but it very well might be the best thing for us when it comes to relying on accumulating "stuff" to bring happiness.

Don't let guilt make you feel obligated to buy all they want.

It's good for grandchildren of all ages too. The *I wannas* and *I've gotta haves* seem to be a way grandkids can take advantage of grandparents' good natures. After all, we like to be their heroes. We like to provide what they want. If you don't have the money for a requested item, be candid about it. Offer to match funds and go half on the item if they will agree to earn their share. Just don't let guilt make you feel obligated to buy all they want. You'll be doing your grandchildren a great favor if you can help them understand that good things are worth waiting for.

Begin in your own heart. Cultivate contentment. Walk around your home and praise God for His sheltering you, instead of seeing every item that needs to be replaced or refurbished. Keep your focus on Christ instead of the stuff! *"Better is a little with the fear of the LORD, than great treasure with trouble"* (Proverbs 15:16).

I know that verse to be true. I remember the stress and weariness that deep debt brought to my heart and marriage. It has taken learning the hard way to *"in whatever state I am, to be content"* (Philippians 4:11). No, it's not easy to forgo buying every darling outfit or newest toy or latest DVD on the shelf, especially at the holidays. However, failure to count the cost often leads to disaster.

I think I'm a pretty typical grandmother when I say I like to buy fun things for my grands, but with a little forethought and ingenuity, living within our means is possible...even with grandchildren. Sweet one, make whatever adjustments or sacrifices that are necessary to manage your money so that you become a good steward of what God has provided for you. We are all prone to compare ourselves with others or want more than we have. Contentment comes from God and being dependent upon Him.

All of our money actually belongs to God in the first place; the sooner we learn that, the better. It is a fallacy to think that accumulating material things leads to contentment. *"Watch out!"* Jesus said. *"Be on guard against all kinds of greed; a man's life does not consist in the abundance of his possessions"* (Luke 12:15 NIV).

Self-indulgent living, purchasing unnecessary things, and succumbing to buying things not in your budget just to please people can cause much unneeded tension in a family. God wants us to depend upon Him, not our material possessions. Our lives, our assets, our time, our families—are all from Him. We are responsible to God for them and God will hold us accountable. Jesus's parable of the talents in Matthew 25:14–30 underscores this principle.

How can we learn to *"set your mind on things above"*? (Colossians 3:2). A good way is to value what God values. Throughout the pages of Scripture, God reminds us that He values people above possessions. He values His Word. People and His Word—those are things that last forever.

> My grandparents were not rich. They didn't win my love by giving me expensive gifts. In fact, a typical Christmas present was a pair of socks. But they gave me something far more valuable than any tangible possession. They gave me love and time.
> —Phil Waldrep, *The Grandparent Factor*

Jesus said, *"Lay up for yourselves treasures in heaven, where neither moth nor rust destroys and where thieves do not break in and steal"* (Matthew 6:20).

The strongest bond to secure family ties with your grandchildren is based on love, not on things. Giving love, we can never go wrong.

LIVING A HOLY HERITAGE WITH ETERNAL VALUES

Whatever your circumstances, you can continue to pass eternal values on to your grandchildren by applying these power-packed principles that I've summed up as follows:

1. Seize every moment. Take time to listen, even when it means putting aside an important task, the newspaper, or a TV show.
2. Make time with each grandchild alone, when possible. Share your family history with each one.
3. Pray for and with your grands, and read the Bible with them. Make a picture prayer journal. Be a student of the Word and pass on the truths by reading *The Children's Bible in 365 Stories* or other illustrated resources to children.
4. Be consistent in your lifestyle, carrying out values in life that you teach. If you teach truthfulness but you are caught in lies, you will pass on the opposite of what you hope to impart.
5. Attend church.
6. Be involved in your grandchildren's lives. Rearrange schedules if need be to attend graduations, recitals, holiday events. Call, write letters, email, or talk to them every week (at least leave messages or instant messages with your teens).
7. Let go of the past! Let it die, never to be resurrected. Give situations to God, once and for all time. Forgive and let go. Mend some fences.
8. Let your life send a message of unconditional love to your grandchildren.
9. Have some fun! Leave loving, laughing memories. Don't forget to smile.
10. Remember this: Everything we do can be a platform for honoring God and advancing His kingdom in the lives of our grandchildren; everyday moments can become teachable moments.

A good man leaves an inheritance to his children's children.
—Proverbs 13:22

We cannot live our lives alone,
For other lives we touch
Are either strengthened by our own,
Or weakened just as much.
—Anonymous

MAKE A DIFFERENCE— AND LET THEM WATCH

16

"I take advantage of talking to God, thanking Him out loud at mealtimes, because those are the only times my grandchildren ever hear anyone pray," says faithful Grandma Charlene. "They see me on my knees praying; they see me studying Scripture, and we talk about the Bible at bedtime when they stay at our home. I keep each one of their pictures among the fruit in our fruit bowl on our breakfast table. Every morning I ask the Lord to fill my grandchildren with a specific trait of the fruit of the Holy Spirit—gentleness, kindness, joy, love, and so on."

Simply put, that's what those verses in Deuteronomy 6:4–9 mean. Living out a faith in our Lord throughout the day so that our grands can *see* what it means to walk humbly with God. They won't just hear about Him from a pulpit—they can watch the practices and attitudes of Jesus lived out before them through their grandmother's life. All our days are made up of potentially memorable moments if we just take the time to make them worth remembering. So many scriptural truths are found in the details; in the day-to-day.

To be sure, let's remember that we cannot give our grandchildren something we do not possess first ourselves, a life thoroughly committed to Christ. No matter where you are in your spiritual walk today, take some time to assess by holding up your life in a spiritual mirror. Do you like what you see? It's good from time to time for all of us to rebuild our Bible reading habits and prayer priorities, and just to have a good, old-fashioned time of rededication of our lives unto the Lord.

Fortunately for the Apostle Paul's young spiritual protégé, Timothy, his mother and grandmother were committed to living faithfully to teach their child and grandchild the truths of the faith. The Book of 2 Timothy does not say that Timothy's mother and grandmother were perfect. Neither are we. But, we can follow their example and lead in our younger generation's spiritual development. I imagine that's why Paul referred to Eunice, Timothy's grandmother. He admonishes us to take heed of the powerfully important influence of a godly grandmother in the life of even one little child and how far-reaching our spiritual influence can be. We must not forget that.

Eternity is at stake. We can help even our young grandchildren understand that salvation comes only by faith in Christ, that it is possible because Jesus lived without sin and willingly died to pay for the sins of all who confess Him as Savior. How wonderful it is when one of our grandchildren accepts Christ as Savior as a young child. What joy we have in our hearts! Such joy must match that of the angels in heaven!

"I pray every day that God will keep my granddaughters close to Him and that they will make a commitment for Christ at a young age. I pray for the temptations and pressures they encounter in their friendships now that they have begun school. I especially pray that they will be kept from evil," said Ruth, a grandmom of five. She went on to say that she places her grandchildren's names in the "Jabez prayer," paraphrasing it for each grandchild. We each can use this prayer as a model:

Jabez called on the God of Israel saying, "Oh, that You would bless me indeed, and enlarge my territory, that . . . You would keep me from evil, that I may not cause pain!" So God granted him what he requested.
—1 Chronicles 4:10

Since Satan's nature is to deceive, it is a great idea to pray protection from the enemy's deception from the time children are small, especially into their young adult years.

My dad gave his first testimony, through his tears, of the forgiveness and salvation he had just received. Willis was crying, too. So was my grandmother. She had prayed unceasingly for more than seven years. God answered the prayers of my grandmother by putting a key person at the critical crossroads.
—James Dobson, *Parenting Isn't for Cowards*

Take Your Grandchildren Stargazing

Making mac and cheese...washing clothes...trying to get a toddler down for a nap...or off of the slide at the park. Whew! God knows that I sometimes lose perspective of the high calling He has given me to care for my young grandchildren while their mommy and daddy go to work and serve in ministry. Sometimes the mundane routines and constant demands to meet needs can become overwhelming, even discouraging. Can you identify? Are you nodding?

The Lord gave me a verse on a card (thank you, Alice!) to place at the top of my refrigerator that I might be visually reminded daily of my service to the Lord when I'm caring for grandchildren. It shows a young boy drinking from a cup that an older person is holding up to his little mouth with a verse printed right underneath the picture. It's been a great inspiration for me to keep on, keeping on. I think Jesus may have had busy grandmoms or moms in mind when He spoke these words: *"'For I was hungry and you gave Me food; I was thirsty, and you gave Me drink.'* ... *'Assuredly, I say to you, inasmuch as you did it unto one of the least of these My brethren, you did it to Me'"* (Matthew 25:35, 40).

> *I think Jesus may have had busy grandmoms or moms in mind when he spoke these words in Matthew 25:35, 40.*

It is remarkable that Jesus counts our service to our little ones a holy offering unto Himself. Every sippy cup of juice we fill and each fruit-drink stained mouth we wipe, often a dozen-plus times a day...all are counted as acts of worship unto our Lord.

Lee Hill-Nelson, a Texas grandmother, encourages us to take moments as simple as looking at the enormous sky with millions of twinkling stars and making them a time to talk about God's creation with our grandchildren. She spreads a blanket on the lawn at nightfall; then asks her grands if they can count the stars. As they gaze up into the sky Lee talks about God and His vast creation from the North Star to the Milky Way to the Big and Little Dippers.

Lee quotes Psalm 147:4: *He counts the number of the stars; He calls them all by name.* What a wonderful way to take a grand tour of God's creation! Grandma Lee has found a beautiful, visual way to instill in her grandchildren just how big God is.

I plan to do the same with my kiddos this next summer at our first Camp Grandma. We'll have a front seat for the show right in my own backyard. We could eat star-shaped cookies we've made earlier in the day while gazing up at the constellations. I want to share with my grands that God is omnipresent—He's everywhere at the same time. And that the same stars my little ones gaze at in Missouri are the very same stars I see where I live. God is watching over us all at the same time—wow. God is so awesome; it's hard to take it all in! Maybe we'll even purchase some packets of glow-in-the dark stars that will adhere to the bedroom ceiling or use them to stick on our hands, cheeks, and arms. I think I'll get some colored foil stars and we can make our own star pictures on black construction paper. We'll have a glowing good time! I'll be sure to let you know how it goes.

Great is the LORD *and most worthy of praise; his greatness no one can fathom.*
—Psalm 145:3 (NIV)

When I talked to my daughter Missy about this chapter, she agreed 100 percent to the idea that it is the little unplanned things that happen in life that afford us opportunities to teach children spiritual lessons if we just take the time to do so. Missy reminded me of several examples that came to her mind about how she goes about working God's attributes into daily living. You might get ideas from what she said:

- When seeing birds in the sky or trees, we talk about where they go through the day and where they fly at night (to their nest) and how God takes care of them. Then we talk of ways He takes good care of us too.
- We talk about how God is always with us, even when we can't see Him. At night when Mommy and Daddy hear a cry, they come help out because they are near. God is always here too.
- We talk about God when it rains because it helps the grass grow.
- At nighttime, we mention that God made the night because He knows we need our rest in order to play and have fun tomorrow.

Those are great examples, aren't they? See how simple, yet how good it is to discover ways to bring God into our grandchildren's lives? We get highbrow ideas about what God is looking for us to do, when it's really very simple. "The job of a grandmother," someone has said, "is bringing little saints to God." That's really what transforms mundane work into that of doing the work of the Lord. Make an offering of your work to God as you stand at your sink and peel those potatoes or wash those dishes. As you go upstairs to clean the ring out of the tub one more time, put some muscle into it. Polish the chrome on that faucet as shiny as you can! It is spiritual work you're doing when you do it as unto the Lord. It is no less spiritual to peel an onion for a nice dinner for your family than it is to lead a Bible study or a 100-voice choir at church. There is nothing more spiritual than the work of God that He has given *you* to do. Your act of spiritual worship is the faithful performance of the duties that God has given *you*. We all would do well to remember: Some days our most important pulpit is right at our own kitchen sink.

> If you want joy for half an hour, take a bubble bath.
> If you want joy for an afternoon, go shopping.
> If you want joy for an evening, go out to dinner.
> If you want joy for a day, kidnap your husband and go on a picnic.
> If you want joy for a week, go on vacation.
> If you want joy for a month, spend within your budget.
> If you want joy for life, invest time in others.
> —Barbara Johnson, *Mama, Get the Hammer!*

LET KIDS SEE WHAT IS IMPORTANT TO YOU

Openly demonstrate your spiritual priority by being faithful to your Bible and devotions. Keep your Bible out on the end table next to the recliner or on the top of your desk. Let your grandkids see that the pages are marked, tattered, and cellophane tape holds some of them together. That's how my mother-in-law's Bible is. I cherish having it in my possession even more than the lovely pieces of jewelry she gave to me just before she passed away. Both are meaningful, and I appreciate her giving them to me, but there's just something about reading Mom's Bible. I love the notes scratched in the margins and specific underlined verses that were beloved to her.

What will your grandchildren learn about you when your Bible is passed down to your family members?

What will your grandchildren learn about you when your Bible is passed down to your family members? The night before the foundation was poured for our home four years ago, Rob and I went over to the property to pray together. We prayed for God to protect and guide the workers all along the way. We asked God to make this a home that would be a welcoming, loving place to all those who enter. We then placed a Bible that Rob had given me in the early years of our marriage down into the moorings. When the cement was poured the next day, we knew our home's was literally built upon the Word of God. We love showing friends and family that visit where my Bible is underneath our bedroom floor. The Word of God is a sure foundation to build any house upon!

It doesn't take kids long to see what's important to their grandmom. Tell your grandkids how you came to accept Jesus Christ into your heart as Savior. How *did* you come to the Lord? What *is* your personal testimony? The opportunities to touch grandchildren with the love of Jesus are unlimited. Here are some ways we can make this work for us while just living our lives:

- Share how Christ has made such an awesome difference in your life.
- Open up about what habits you've conquered, fears He's erased, worries eased, and how relationships have been healed. Tell how your life changed direction when the Lord became the center of your life. Share about a time at youth camp or in your teens at youth group when you dedicated your life to Christ.
- Let your grandchildren know by hearing your stories. Talk about how God is presently working in your life.
- Fill them in on countless answers to prayer.
- Read the Bible together.
- Demonstrate your faith during the week, not just on Sunday. If their parents allow, take your grandchildren to church regularly. If they are in your home for a visit, make it a habit that they know you'll be going to church on Sunday because that's what you always do. Have prayers at mealtimes; slow down enough to hold hands.
- Play Christian music around the house and hum your favorites. (Teens will act annoyed, but trust me, you're making memories they'll cherish.)
- Bless your children with compliments on their character through touch, words, smiles, and lots of praise. No grandkid ever outgrows the need for hugs!
- Introduce Christian heroes of yours to older grandchildren through biographies and testimonies in DVDs.
- Explain clearly what Easter and Christmas mean to you. Have some appropriate Scriptures for the holiday to read, prayers to offer, and time to reflect on Jesus, His birthday, and that He is our Savior.
- Give gifts with spiritual meaning and purpose. Give a devotional book—the same as yours so you both are reading the same devotion

each day. Read good books aloud to young children and even preteens. You can never read too much to a child. Never ever.

- Give spiritual answers (not sermons) when they ask questions. Plant God's truth in their hearts—someday it will make sense and "click" for them. God's Word never returns void.

What a difference you can make, precious grandmom, in the lives of your grandchildren!

Grandmothers, you and I are called on to pass on to another generation our faith stories. The greatest inheritance you can leave is your faith.
—Esther Burroughs, *Treasures of a Grandmother's Heart*

PRIORITIZE PURITY

17

Building a strong spiritual legacy for your grandchildren requires planning and commitment, but the rewards in eternity are well worth it. As someone once said, "We are always one generation away from atheism." Make a considered commitment to be the one person your grandchildren can always count on for spiritual values. Get involved in your children's lives; do whatever it takes. There will be times when you are discouraged and tempted to give up; but stay involved in their activities and interests, no matter what. You are building a spiritual legacy... line upon line, precept upon precept.

In this "no values" culture that our grandchildren are growing up in, teaching morality and purity is paramount. Our grandchildren may not get that teaching if it is not from us grandmoms. Today's world message is: If it feels good, go for it. Do your own thing. And many of our grandkids are going to do just that for a while—their *own* thing. Some things our grandchildren wear and do will leave us scratching our heads. Promise yourself you will not bring out your heaviest KJV Bible and throw it at them! Patience, tolerance, and a divine closing of our mouths will, in the long run, serve much better. That's how we earn the right to speak up later.

Pray Proverbs 31 over your granddaughters. *Virtuous* and *purity* are certainly not words seen in today's magazines for teen girls, nor do they reflect the world's view of sexuality. Preoccupation with sex has absolutely permeated our culture. I am continually shocked at what is accepted as the norm in the areas of dress, media, television, and in our sex-crazed society in general. By displaying modesty ourselves in our dress and proper priorities with regard to our body image, our granddaughters will see the kind of beauty God gives—a kind of beauty that is certainly not found in slick magazines.

Do you not know that your body is the temple of the Holy Spirit who is in you, whom you have from God, and you are not your own? For you were bought at a price; therefore glorify God in your body and in your spirit, which are God's.
—1 Corinthians 6:19–20

Let your teenage grandkids hear you being thankful and respecting your body—aches, pains, and jiggles, whether you are skinny or fat. Jokingly we can talk about what sags or is now flapping in the breeze that did not used to, but there is a deep-seated need for young women today to see older women who live out contentment in every area of our lives, especially where appearance is concerned. All the makeover shows in the world cannot give satisfaction unless Christ does the true, ultimate makeover in our hearts.

Our bodies belong to God. Romans 12:1–2 tells us that we are to *"present your bodies a living sacrifice,"* to do His will and further His kingdom in the way that honors and glorifies Him. Grandmothers who dress with dignity earn the respect of their grandchildren. We can still dress in style, very much so. But, it is a wise woman who is perceptive enough to realize that certain clothes designed for teens are not suited for the 40-, 50-, or 60-something in public.

> *Grandmothers who dress with dignity earn the respect of their grandchildren. We can still dress in style.*

While it may not fall under your "job description" as a grandmother at this time, if there is not a teen granddaughter in your life right now, you still can reinforce modest behavior and give direction when you have opportunity. If you have a young granddaughter, when the two of you are together alone, share with her your confidence that she is a princess of God. Discuss the importance of modesty and purity, and how you know it is hard to do the right thing when it seems that everyone else is doing the wrong thing. Tell her again that she is special to God, and special to you. Encourage her to think about her own standards, what type of woman she wants to be, and then to live up to her ideals. Be gentle, but be clear about where you stand on these issues. Praise her for specific instances when her dress has been appropriate. Tell her how pretty she is. Continue your loving affirmations as she grows into young womanhood.

Give your granddaughter a gift certificate for her birthday and go shopping with her. Have an honest conversation with her while you take a snack break. It is our responsibility to speak up! Let older granddaughters hear how males clearly think differently than we women do. I know many young women have thought twice before surrendering to premarital sex because they knew how important their purity was in the heart of their grandmother. Even if it wasn't important to her parents, a godly grandmother's opinion is very influential to a teen girl who would never want to have to make the phone call to Grams to tell her she was pregnant.

You can talk frankly to your granddaughter about how you know temptations are tough. Let her see that you know a thing or two, that you had the same temptations when dating as she is having. Let her hear the sad consequences and guilt from decisions many girls make believing a guy is really interested in them when truth is, he just wants sex. Let her know you understand how hard it is to say no. But, also let her know that with true love and commitment in marriage, sex can have its full beauty. That's God's plan.

Since your teen granddaughter (and grandson) is hearing from peers, television, and movies that sex is the way to winning a date, speak up and say that sexual surrender is not the way to win a guy—at least, not one worth having. A wonderful mate is worth the wait! Knowing she'll have gratitude and respect from her Mr. Right in the future will make it a little easier to abstain right now. Help her to keep that thought ever-present in her mind.

One young couple I know had dated seriously for over a year. They were getting involved sexually and realized they had to come to a halt or suffer heartbreaking consequences. Determined to restrain their feelings from getting too carried away, they began keeping their Bible placed on the car seat between them on every date for a whole month. Tell your grandsons and granddaughters about this couple's drastic measure, and encourage them to apply it!

Barb Trosclair, one "happening" grandma, gave me a wonderful idea when she did a workshop on making Purity Bracelets. I went to her class and came away with a darling bracelet that I'd made myself, with Barb's help, of course. (Yes, I'll confess—I'm very craft-challenged!) We threaded pearls together on clear fishing line, and then we each got to choose one very unique bead and one ruby-colored bead to add to our bracelets. Barb talked about what each represented. There were pearls so that each girl would be reminded that she is "a pearl of great price" to God. The bead that was different from anyone else's would stand for how God made her special, unlike anyone else. The red bead signified the virtuous Proverbs 31 woman who is worth "far above rubies."

I'm so glad I got to make a bracelet. It has inspired me to make one with my granddaughters when they are older. I hope you will too. Barb showed us how she gave each of her granddaughters a little note on a card that showed what the bracelet represented. The response from the girls making them in our class was terrific, and I just know your granddaughters would love making one too. What a wonderful way to teach and talk about purity to a young woman in a life of maturing and growing in Christ.

> Acceptance is an important secret grandparents can share with grandkids. My wife tells how her grandmother taught her by example to accept and love those with physical deformities. She learned not to laugh at an old man's stoop, nor shun a person with a missing limb, nor tease a child who stutters.
> —Eric Wiggin, *The Gift of Grandparenting*

ALL MY LOVE AND ALL MY KISSIN'

Affirmation has great value. Just as you might say to your grandchild, *You had real character when you gave back the $10 bill that clerk accidentally gave you,* affirms honesty, so does what you have to say regarding dating, fashions, and friendships. Affirmation builds trust, fosters communication, and cherishes security for any grandchild.

Dear grandmom, fashion and styles are not worth losing a love relationship with your grandchild over. I know of several grandparents who have taken in a teen grandchild for a few months, or even a few years, as the grandchild went through those rough, turbulent teen years. One such example is Robyn, who was haunted by the ghosts of her parents' quarreling and divorce and was left feeling unwanted. Here's what Grandmom Genevieve in Kansas told me: "We took Robyn into our home because she needed someone of blood relation to care for her. So we opened our home to let her know that no matter what, we would always cherish her and she'd never be alone without family. Only the acceptance of our love and God's redemption can heal these wounds. It will take time for her to heal and we will be here for her as long as it takes."

> She could not speak, but she did "hold on," and the warm grasp of the friendly hand comforted her sore heart, and seemed to lead her nearer to the Divine arm which alone could uphold her in her trouble.
> —Louisa May Alcott, *Little Women*

No fanfare. Just commitment to what they felt God needed them to do. They looked beyond the tattoos, belly-button piercing, and made a difference in their granddaughter's life. No matter what. During that time, this elderly, godly Meemaw and Pawpaw communicated unconditional acceptance, affection, and affirmation that washed away any of Robyn's doubts if someone loved her. They did it for her good; they did it to keep a love relationship with her; they did it in obedience to God. They never gave up. As for Robyn, it was impossible to be in the presence of grandparents who love both her and Jesus dearly and not be changed drastically.

Every day this precious set of grandparents was able to handle their trial with God's grace. I watched, as week after week, Robyn came into our teen class, often reluctant and rebellious, her attitude trying unsuccessfully to disguise her need for love. She had so many abandonment issues; after all, neither her mom nor her dad cared about her.

One of the things her grandparents did right was to not force and push on issues that did not matter in light of eternity. They clung to Isaiah 46:4:

> "Even to your old age, I am He,
> And even to gray hairs I will carry you!
> I have made, and I will bear;
> Even I will carry, and will deliver you."

I learned that Robyn's dear grandmom covered a shoe box with spray paint and called it a "God Box." Fashioned like a Valentine's Day box with a slit in the top, she placed a stack of index cards beside the God Box on the kitchen counter. When the grandparents or Robyn would have a worry, each would write the care on an index card and slide it into the God Box. This was a physical, visual way for them to recognize that they were giving their cares over to the Lord. What a great idea from these grandparents! Simple, yet it worked. Over and over when an anxious thought through the day would arise back into her mind, Robyn would remind herself that she had already placed that care into God's hands. It was in the God Box, and He was big enough to take care of it. From talking to an awful lot of grandmothers, I'm convinced that with all the trials and worries about grandchildren out there, a lot grandmoms (and grandchildren!) would benefit a great deal from a God Box.

BESTOW AN ETERNAL HERITAGE

18

I have many fond memories of my growing up years. I don't remember much from the preschool years. I do remember that we had a large weeping willow tree between our house and our grandpa's filling station. I spent lots of time playing under the tree. We had a homemade swing in the backyard, and we all spent time sitting in the yard in metal lawn chairs. People would drive by and see us in the yard as they went to the filling station and would stop to visit with us.

We went to church in the town of West Salem. It had a very small congregation and few children. We had children's Sunday School in the basement. We sat on little red chairs. Mom tied my offering in the corner of a handkerchief. I was saved and baptized when I was in the eighth grade. We were having a revival and the invitation song was "Almost Persuaded." I remember it well.

Mom made many of my clothes. We would go shopping and I would pick out clothes I liked, then she would go home and make them for me. I liked what she made as no one else ever had clothes like mine. One dress that she made I wore to a dance at our high school. It was red taffeta with a harem skirt and a red-and-white cummerbund. I had a red-and-white checked handkerchief to match. I had handkerchiefs that matched many of my dresses.

It was at church that I met Tom. He called on a Monday night

to ask me out for the following weekend, and I said yes. We went to the Fox Theater in St. Louis and saw the movie *To Kill a Mockingbird;* then we ate at the Pancake House. Right from the beginning we saw each other almost every night of the week or talked on the phone. We became engaged on my birthday in August, not quite five months after we began dating."
—Mary Ellen Richards Martens

This intriguing story makes me want to hear the "rest of the story," as commentator Paul Harvey would have said. It is a segment of the life story of Mary Ellen Richards Martens. The Martenses are not a famous family. You've probably never heard of them. But the story and album containing pictures that correspond with it are all very important to Mindy and Rick Martens, my daughter and son-in-love. That's because the handwritten story is from Rick's mother, Mary Ellen, given to him several Christmases ago. Rick will cherish it always as one of his most prized possessions now and later to pass down to his three daughters. (Have I mentioned that these three are among the best, brightest, and most adorable three little girls in the whole wide world?)

> Whatever you may know of your family's past, especially its Christian heritage, can help give your grandchildren a sense of who they are and a sense of direction for the coming years.
> —Eric Wiggin, *The Gift of Grandparenting*

Mary Ellen's information spans more than 100 years—newspaper clippings, copies of death certificates, roots, her family's place in history. If Mary Ellen had not penned them, Rick would not have these valuable stories to pass down. Some of the information in the book he read or was hearing about for the first time ever.

As I read through Mary Ellen's painstakingly accurate recordings of her history, I knew I wanted to carry on the tradition so my adult children would have my side of the family to pass down, too. I went right out and bought a binder to begin. Everything I've gathered isstill in manila envelopes, but it will get done, by and by. Even though my life story would never be the screenplay for a movie, it is one I wish to transfer on to my children, down to great-great-grandchildren and beyond. It is a story that is important to *us.*

God Himself admonishes us to learn from our previous generations. He indicates that it is important to remember: *"Only take heed to yourself and diligently keep yourself, lest you forget the things your eyes have seen, and lest they depart from your heart all the days of your life. And teach them to your children and your grandchildren"* (Deuteronomy 4:9).

We all need to be recording our family stories. It's one thing to tell tales aloud, but quite another to have them recorded all in one place with photos. Seeing Mary Ellen's work helped me understand how meaningful it could be to have family stories all together in one book.

> God seems to expect one generation to learn from the previous one. He does not intend to have to re-teach every lesson, and is counting on that heritage to be passed down from family to family.
> —Stephen and Janet Bly, *The Power of a Godly Grandparent*

You can do it! Get to work on your family story. Your work doesn't have to be work for editorial scrutiny. Just write your own words, your own way. Let your personality come through by the way you express yourself and how you describe family descendants. Use ink that will not fade and invest in a nicely bound journal that is acid free. Treat your family stories like the treasure they are. Your children and grandchildren and beyond will thank you.

Make sure future generations know their spiritual heritage along with their family tree. Since my birth mother died when I was so young, I've had to ask questions of her relatives for information to fill in my history gaps on that side of the family. I've loved meeting people who are not relatives, as well, who have told me stories of going to high school with my mother and how she was influential in their coming to know the Lord as Savior.

WALKING DOWN MEMORY LANE

Last fall I was privileged to be the keynote speaker for a women's conference in Girard, Kansas, just minutes from the farm where I lived with my grandparents for a time when my mother was sick and after she passed away. Ann Geir was my host; she's the person who knew my birth mother as a teen. And now look how cool God is to bring us together this many years later to serve the Lord in her church together! Ann told me privately that she just stared at me in amazement as to how I spoke and moved just like my birth mother, June. Somehow, Ann and I both felt we knew my birth mother would be proud.

My daughter Mindy was able to accompany me on this trip so that we could take this walk down memory lane together. It was precious to go to the farm together where I have pictures of me as a three-year-old standing by the water pump and in front of the chicken coop. Then, to stand, arm in arm, at the site where my birth mother and grandmother, Beulah Gray, are buried, was moving beyond words for me.

I'm so thankful, far more than I can pen, for the gift of this trip that God gave Mindy and me together. Family is so important. Family history lets us know where we've been so that we, with pride and renewed courage, can face where we're headed. Believe me, it's more effective to tell your grandkids what life has been like for you if you can take them there.

Have you taken your children and grandchildren to your family's cemetery plots? I don't mean just at funeral time. Have they seen the old homestead? Where you lived as a kid and went to school? Do they know their historical origins? A little here, a little there, our stories and time shared together will be more of a fortune to them than if you had all the wealth of Bill Gates to pass down.

Echoes in Eternity

"What we do in this life echoes in eternity." That powerful statement is made in the movie *Gladiator* by General Maximus Decimus Meridius when he addresses his troops and challenges them to do their very best. He's reminding them that they are not just taking up space on this planet, but have the opportunity at that moment to make an eternal difference with their lives.

So do you! Rise up, grandmom! Be the grandmother God destined you to be! Let the legacy you leave be your life. In the end, when we are at the last of our days, and we look back over our life, what do you think we'll consider the most important of all we did? What will be the job that had the most impact on the generations to come after us? What will we consider to be the most significant thing we spent time on? Doubtful that we'll say we wished we had spent more time watching television, or working out at the gym or shopping.

Right now, today, I challenge you as I challenge myself to think deeply about what is the greatest impact we'll make on this earth in the remaining years we have left. Like you, I've got lots going on in my life—at church, with my girlfriends, in my work as a writer and speaker, with my husband . . . but more and more I'm seeing the eternal difference I can make as a grandmother. If we do that job well, I believe that at the end of our days, we will feel at peace. We will have done the most important work of all—we will have had an impact on the next generation, our grandchildren, for eternity.

BIBLIOGRAPHY

WORKS CITED

Alcott, Louisa May. *Little Women*. New York: Spark Educational Publishing, 2004.

Bly, Stephen and Janet. *The Power of a Godly Grandparent: Leaving a Spiritual Legacy*. Kansas City: Beacon Hill Press, 2003.

Borge, Victor. http://en.wikipedia.org/wiki/Victor_Borge, accessed December 18, 2007.

Burroughs, Esther. *Treasures of a Grandmother's Heart: Finding Pearls of Wisdom in Everyday Moments*. Birmingham: New Hope Publishers 2002.

Criswell, W. A. Quoted by Vernon C. Grounds in *Our Daily Bread* online, April 26, 2007, http://www.rbc.org/odb/odb-04-26-07.shtml.

Dean, Jennifer Kennedy. *Legacy of Prayer: A Spiritual Trust Fund for the Generations*. Birmingham: New Hope Publishers, 2002.

Dickinson, Emily. "I Shall Not Live in Vain." In *Collected Poems of Emily Dickinson*. Avenel, NJ: Gramercy Books.

Dobson, James. *Parenting Isn't for Cowards: Dealing Confidently with the Frustrations of Child-Rearing*. Waco, TX: Word Books, 1987.

Dobson, James. *Focus on the Family* radio program. www.fotf.org.

Dreschnack, Edward H. http://thinkexist.com/quotes/with/keyword/grandmother.

Elgin, Suzette Haden. *The Grandmother Principles*. New York: Abbeville Press, 1998.

Elliot, Elisabeth. Interview from *Back to the Bible* radio segment *Gateway to Joy*. http://www.backtothebible.org/gateway-to-joy/ideas-for-grandmothers.html.

Graham, Billy. *Hope for the Troubled Heart*. Minneapolis: Grayson Publishing, 1991.

Haddix, Deborah. http://www.extendedlegacy.com.

Haley, Alex. Quoted in *Long Distance Grandma* by Janet Teitsort. Louisiana Howard Publishing.

Johnson, Barbara. *Mama, Get the Hammer! There's a Fly on Papa's Head!* Dallas: Word Publishing, 1994.

Kitzinger, Sheila. *Becoming a Grandmother: A Life Transition*.

Lewis, C. S. *The Problem of Pain*. San Francisco: HarperSanFransico, 2001.

Littauer, Florence. *The Gift of Encouraging Words*. Dallas: Word Publishing, 1995.

McCullough, Mamie. *Get It Together: And Remember Where You Put It*. Dallas: W Publishing Group, 1991.

Naessens, Grace L. "No Time to Pray." No copyright, available various online sources. See http://inspire.luquette.org/the_difference.htm.

Otto, Donna. *The Gentle Art of Mentoring*. Eugene, OR: Harvest House Publishers, 1997.

Perret, Gene. http://www.quotegarden.com/grandparents.html, accessed December 18, 2007.

Peters, Angie. *Celebrate Home: Great Ideas for Stay-At-Home Moms*. St. Louis: Concordia Publishing House, 1998.

Peterson, Eugene. *The Message*. Colorado Springs: Navpress Publishing Group, 2002.

Scott, Willard. *If I Knew It Was Going to Be This Much Fun, I Would Have Become a Grandparent First*. New York: Hyperion, 2004.

Sutterfield, Ken. *The Power of an Encouraging Word*. Green Forest, AR: New Leaf Press, 1997.

Waldrep, Phil. *The Grandparent Factor: Five Principles to Help You Make a Difference in the Life of Your Grandchild*. Friendswood, TX: Baxter Press, 2003.

Warren, Rick. *The Purpose-Driven Life*. Grand Rapids, MI: Zondervan, 2002.

Wiggin, Eric. *The Gift of Grandparenting: Building Meaningful Relationships with Your Grandchildren*. Carol Stream, IL: Tyndale House Publishers, 2001. A Focus on the Family book.

Zemke, Dawn. "The Gift of Gratitude." *Today's Christian Woman*, January/February 2008, 52–54.

New Hope® Publishers is a division of WMU®,
an international organization that challenges Christian believers
to understand and be radically involved in God's mission.
For more information about WMU, go to www.wmu.com.
More information about New Hope books may be found
at www.newhopepublishers.com. New Hope books
may be purchased at your local bookstore.

Books For the Rest of the Trip

Treasures of a Grandmother's Heart
*Finding Pearls of Wisdom
in Everyday Moments*
Esther Burroughs
978-1-56309-722-2

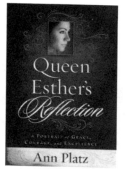

Queen Esther's Reflection
*A Portrait of Grace,
Courage, and Excellence*
Ann Platz
978-1-59669-012-7

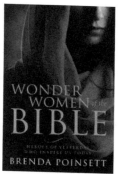

Wonder Women of the Bible
*Heroes of Yesterday
Who Inspire Us Today*
Brenda Poinsett
978-1-59669-094-3

Born to Be Wild
Rediscover the Freedom of Fun
Jill Baughan
978-1-59669-048-8

Available in bookstores everywhere

For information about these books or any New Hope product visit www.newhopepublishers.com.